GOLFING
WITH DAD

Also by David Barrett:

Golf Magazine's Golf Rules Explained
Golf Courses of the U.S. Open
Golf's Dream 18s
Miracle at Merion
The PGA Championship: 1916–1985 (contributor)
Golf In America: The First 100 Years (contributor)
Golf The Greatest Game: The USGA Celebrates
Golf In America (contributor)
20th Century Golf Chronicle (contributor)
Golf Legends Of All Time (contributor)
Wit & Wisdom of Golf (contributor)
Best of Golf (contributor)
These Guys Are Good (contributor)
The Love of Golf (contributor)

THE GAME'S GREATEST PLAYERS REFLECT ON
THEIR FATHERS AND THE GAME THEY LOVE

GOLFING WITH DAD

DAVID BARRETT

Skyhorse Publishing

Skyhorse Publishing books may be purchased in bulk at special discounts for sales promotion, corporate gifts, fund-raising, or educational purposes. Special editions can also be created to specifications. For details, contact the Special Sales Department, Skyhorse Publishing, 307 West 36th Street, 11th Floor, New York, NY 10018 or info@skyhorsepublishing.com.

Skyhorse® and Skyhorse Publishing® are registered trademarks of Skyhorse Publishing, Inc.®, a Delaware corporation.

www.skyhorsepublishing.com

10 9 8 7 6 5 4 3 2 1

Library of Congress Cataloging-in-Publication Data is available on file.
ISBN: 978-1-61608-253-6

Printed in the United States of America

For Dad

Contents

Introduction

This book tells the stories of fourteen tour pros and their fathers and how golf shaped and influenced their relationship. I am decidedly not a tour pro, and not even a low-handicapper, though I did once get down to single digits for four weeks. My late father — Dave Sr. — didn't play golf when I was growing up. Yet our golf story is, in its own way, pretty compelling.

There are two reasons my dad didn't play golf until he was nearly forty years old. First, he wasn't exposed to the game when he was growing up. Second, he had a bad back. A really bad back. The problems started in his early twenties and involved separate injuries or ailments in his lower, middle, and upper back. The twisting and turning of a golf swing were out of the question. Or so it seemed.

So, I wasn't exposed to golf either. But I loved sports, as both a fan and a participant. From the ages of six to twelve, I practically lived and breathed baseball, while finding plenty of time for basketball and football too. When I was twelve, I began to be intrigued by golf. My cousin Rich wanted to learn to play — his dad was an occasional weekend golfer. We didn't really have anybody to teach us, so we learned on our own by hitting plastic balls in his backyard.

One thing that enriched the golf scene in those days was an abundance of pitch-and-putt courses where kids could be introduced to the game (sadly lacking in most places today). For our first golf outing, my mom dropped us off at a pitch-and-putt. We brought our entire sets of clubs with us—my dad had bought me a used set. Rich pulled out his driver on the hundred-yard first hole. "Great shot!" I enthused as his ball took off straight, a low line drive that landed short of the green—and proceeded to roll about forty yards past it.

I soon graduated to a regular course for my first round at age twelve. By the time I was fourteen, my summer was filled with golf. My next-door neighbor Paul and I spent several days a week at the Plainfield West Nine in New Jersey. This was a public course owned by and across the street from the renowned Plainfield Country Club.

The West Nine was a poorer cousin, a nine-hole, 2,500-yard, par-33 public course with a modest green fee—in short, a perfect place for two young kids to play. It wasn't crowded, so, playing as a twosome, we typically tooled around for forty-five or fifty-four holes. The first eighteen were pretty much just warming up.

As I got older, my small size caught up to me in other sports. I went from a Little League star to a Pony League mediocrity and didn't make the ninth-grade basketball team. I was a cocaptain of the freshman soccer team—but before tenth grade we moved to Durham, North Carolina, where at the time (1971) there was no high school soccer.

I was left with just golf and threw myself into it with a passion. I was a serviceable no. 4 player on a pretty good high school golf team and became a fanatic follower of the PGA Tour. My parents and I watched the tournaments on television every week and my friend Sam and I pored over each week's issue of *Golf World* to see who made it through Monday qualifying—we were even more fascinated with the tour's "rabbits" than we were with the stars.

My father saw my enthusiasm for golf. When I was fifteen, he gave me the best Christmas present I ever got—a new set of golf clubs that was absolutely a complete surprise. By the time my high school years were nearing their end, his interest in the game had been thoroughly piqued by all the golf talk and golf watching. Instead of the son being brought into the game by the father, it was the other way around.

But there was the matter of Dad's back problems. He could only manage a half backswing and his golf aspirations didn't extend beyond pitch-and-putt. Neither of us dreamed that he would do anything more than that.

In fact, I wasn't sure that he would stick with it for very long. Dad had a long history of hobbies that he pursued intensely for a few months before dropping them and moving on to the next one. There was shortwave radio, harmonica playing, air-pistol shooting, calligraphy, and more.

We played a few pitch-and-putt rounds, and thoroughly enjoyed them, before I headed away to college. Dad's interest in golf only grew. He found a driving-range teacher who was willing to work within his physical limitations to improve his ability to hit the ball. Over the course of a series of lessons and other practice sessions at the range, he began to hit the ball farther and became comfortable with hitting all the clubs.

When I came home the next summer, Dad was ready to play on a regulation course. He had to wear a back brace, and his backswing was still not all that much more than halfway. He couldn't reach any of the par fours in two shots or par fives in three. He looked a little funny with his abbreviated swing, but he was not embarrassed. Nor should he have been. He hit the ball straight, was pretty good around the greens, and shot not too much over 100. I'm sure he was proud just to be able to play on a full-length golf course. And I was proud of him too in a sort of reverse father-son way.

But dad didn't stop there. The lessons continued and his game progressed. During the next couple of summers, we played pretty often. Dad was now shooting in the 90s on a fairly short but regulation course. I noticed something odd about my behavior when I played with him. For some reason, I began to display anger after bad shots. I don't recall flinging any clubs, but there were definitely tantrums. What's odd is that I'm a calm person and didn't act that way when I played with others.

My amateur analysis is that I must have wanted him to think of me as a good golfer. I wanted to *show* that I felt I shouldn't be hitting those bad shots — therefore, I must be a good golfer. Or something like that. In any case, he never said anything about it, nor did it detract from his enjoyment of the game, which was palpable.

Dad began to play with a couple of friends from work. By now, he was hitting the ball far enough to be capable of reaching greens in regulation. He had gained enough flexibility that his swing expanded to three-quarters, and he could fit in with golfers who had been playing the game for a long time.

I got a sports writing job in Virginia for a year and then moved on to the *Augusta Chronicle* in Augusta, Georgia. Living out of town, I didn't get to play with dad that often. But I followed his progress from a distance. As a testament to his further development, he began to play at Duke University Golf Course, a longer, hillier course designed by Robert Trent Jones. He joined the Duke Men's Golf Association. He enjoyed going out by himself after work and being paired with whatever strangers happened to be about to go off the first tee. He was a real golfer now, a pretty good one, as I was about to find out firsthand.

On one occasion when my mom and dad visited Augusta three or four years after I got out of college, we played a round at Forest Hills Golf Course, a public layout that is the home course of Augusta State University and was designed by Donald Ross. My dad usually walked when he played, pulling a cart. But this time, my mom, Virginia, came along to watch and rode in a cart with him.

Forest Hills is a tight, tree-lined course that measured about 6,300 yards from the regular tees. Dad had one of his best rounds, shooting, I recall, something like an 86. I didn't play particularly well, but it wasn't a terrible round by any means. I think I shot an 88.

This is where our story intersects with many of those in the book, albeit from an opposite perspective. It's a common theme of the child golfer improving by stages and finally reaching the point where they beat their father for the first time. Only for us, it was father beating the son.

Dad was keeping a scorecard, but he was a one-hole-at-a-time kind of guy who probably was unaware of our cumulative scores. We never had a match going, or anything like that. It wasn't part of our golf dynamic. I always keep my own score in my head—no scorecard needed. I knew dad was playing great, so I probably checked his card at some point late in the round and knew he had a chance to beat me.

Dad finished the round strong. He may not have known the score, but in any case he didn't give me any opening to catch him. When he added up the numbers on the card, he saw that his score was lower than mine.

He acted a little bit sheepish about it, like he thought I wouldn't be happy. In truth, I've never been happier to be beaten on the golf course. His play that day, and his progress in the game, filled me with pride—and still does. When my father first picked up a club, I couldn't imagine his ever being able to hit a golf ball more than one hundred yards. I'm not sure he could imagine it either. But through sheer determination he became a golfer capable of shooting in the mid-80s on a good golf course. That's inspirational. And that was my dad.

Brad Adamonis

B rad Adamonis was just shy of thirty-five when he finally reached the PGA Tour in January 2008. His father, Dave, had been told a little more than two years earlier that he probably had just two months to live, but he made a mockery of that prognosis and fortunately was able to see his son accomplish his dream of reaching the game's highest level.

You couldn't really blame doctors for their grim diagnosis. After all, in the fall of 2005, Dave was battling three forms of cancer at the same time. He lost seventy pounds but fought the disease, and dealt with the complications from surgery, with everything he had, and made a stunning recovery. Dave not only survived, he got back on his feet and was able to return to work and also to watch Brad play on the secondary Nationwide Tour in 2006 and 2007 — even walking the course as Brad's caddie in one event.

While his father was waging that courageous struggle, Brad won a Nationwide Tour tournament in 2007 and made it through Q-School that winter to qualify for the PGA Tour, the culmination of years of perseverance. In 2008, Dave got to watch Brad in person at several PGA Tour events and also to watch on television as his son nearly won a tournament, losing in a play-off at the John Deere Classic.

Of all the horrible luck, Dave came down with yet another form of cancer in the fall of 2008 and passed away a year later at the age of sixty-two. He left behind quite a legacy. In his native Rhode Island, he started an organization that runs junior golf tournaments and founded *Ocean State Golf* magazine — all as a sidelight to his regular job as a schoolteacher. Then he headed down to Miami and started a golf management program at Johnson & Wales University, where he coached the golf team to an NAIA national title.

On a family level, Brad remembers the support he received over the years, from his days learning the game and playing junior tournaments in Rhode Island to the years when his career stalled on the minitours. "I was lucky I had parents who were supportive. Most would have just said, 'Hey, you're not going to make it.'"

Brad was introduced to the game at the age of three when he would ride in the golf cart with his father, who would let him hit some shots. "I even remember one specifically that I hit pretty good, and Dad clapped," Brad says.

Brad seriously got into the game during the summer when he was eight, but not through any plan by his parents, Dave and Roberta. With both of them working, they signed him up for day camp, but Brad hated it. He wanted to play golf with older brother Dave Jr., who was playing every day with a friend.

"I begged my parents to let me go play golf," Brad remembers. "I just basically said, 'I'm not going [to day camp]. You can drop me off there, but I'm walking home.'"

His parents relented, and the golf course became his day camp. He played on weekends too with his father and grandfather. And he even played in a couple of junior tournaments that year. "I think I shot 136 for eighteen holes, with a 69 and 67 on the nines, in my first tournament. I thought it was pretty cool."

Brad's improvement was rapid over the next several years. Encouraged by a former neighbor who had moved to San Diego, Dave brought Brad out west to the Junior World Golf Championships at Torrey Pines. When he was twelve years old, Brad won his age group, a huge accomplishment because the tournament attracted a strong international field.

Brad now fully appreciates the sacrifices his father made so he could play junior golf. His father was a teacher, but he got a second job selling fertilizer to golf courses. Brad would often go along with his dad on his rounds and chip and putt on the practice greens of the various courses while Dave worked on sealing the deal. Dave also had stints at managing a nine-hole course and working as a course superintendent.

"He went above and beyond in giving us opportunities to play," says Brad. "He didn't play much golf when he was hustling to make some bucks so I could play golf. I was playing tournaments around the country, which wasn't very possible for a teacher with three kids [the family also includes a daughter, Kimberly]."

On top of all this, Dave found time to work on his own venture, the US Challenge Cup Junior Golf Foundation, an organization he started in order to give better junior players in New England a chance to play tournaments. He began it in 1980, just when Dave and then Brad were coming along.

"There weren't many junior tournaments in the area back then," Brad says. "He started with one tournament, and by the time I was playing, there were six. Now there are about thirty. It opened the door for kids from New England to be able to get into better colleges and get golf scholarships. And my father started it basically because he loved us and wanted us to have a chance to play more tournaments."

Dave Jr. was a good junior player in his own right, and he's now carrying on his father's legacy by running the Challenge Cup foundation.

Before he curtailed his play, Dave Sr. was a good-enough player to win the Rhode Island Public Links Championship and compete in the Rhode Island Amateur. Brad and Dave Jr. each caddied for him in some of those tournaments; each also took his turn in winning the state Father-Son Championship with Dave Sr.

Brad actually drifted away from golf to a certain extent after turning fifteen, perhaps a little bit burned out after playing just about every day in season for the previous seven years. "I started playing other sports and discovered girls. I just wanted to be a kid, I guess."

No longer a hot college prospect, Adamonis nonetheless managed to get a scholarship at Miami University in Ohio, not a golf powerhouse but a school with a decent program. His fire for the game was rekindled, and he made the All Mid-American Conference first team.

Those credentials didn't stamp him as a can't-miss pro, but upon graduation in 1996, Brad headed down to Florida, determined to make his way in the world of golf. What followed was four years of working at golf courses and playing minitours when he got the chance. During this time, he received steady encouragement from his father, with frequent use of a couple of his favorite catchphrases: PPO for "patience pays off" and PPT for "the power of positive thinking."

In 2000, Dave moved to Florida himself when Johnson & Wales University added a golf-management program at its Miami campus. "He was always into creating new things," says Brad. "He got a lot of players to go who you wouldn't think would go to an NAIA [small-college] school." By 2005, Johnson & Wales won the NAIA Championship.

While Brad credits his father for always having patience and encouraging him to persevere in his golf dreams, there was a time when he sensed that his parents were close to giving up on him making it in pro golf. This was in 2001 when he was twenty-eight and still struggling on the minitours. "I think they were almost telling me to get a job," he says. "They paid for my first four tournaments on the Hooters Tour and said that would be about all they could do. I realized, 'I've got to make it happen now,' and I started playing pretty well."

Adamonis managed to support himself on the Hooters Tour beyond those four tournaments, and at the end of the year he made it to the PGA Tour Qualifying School final stage and qualified for the Buy.com Tour (which became the Nationwide Tour in 2003).

It wasn't quite the breakthrough he hoped for. After three lackluster years on the Buy.com/Nationwide Tour, Adamonis lost his card and found himself without a place to play in 2005. Looking back, he feels that he got too technical with his swing and strayed from his roots. Nor did he listen enough to the swing advice his father gave him during that time.

"I worked with a lot of teachers and got away from what my father taught me," Brad says. "It's too bad I didn't listen to him more. Really, the things he said would have helped me out. I would get caught up in some swing philosophy, and I would say, 'Dad, you don't know what you're talking about.' But he had a fundamental swing.

"I started looking at video of my swing too much. That was the wrong perspective. Do you see Tom Brady watching video and breaking down his arm angle? Dad didn't need video. If I had stuck with his fundamentals, I would have been all right. But he let me make my mistakes and live and learn."

During those three years, Dave would caddie for his son two or three times a year.

"One time it was about 105 degrees in Knoxville," Brad recalls with a chuckle. "I remember he was giving me a hard time saying I had ten water bottles in my bag. And I came back at him saying that the towel was soaking wet so I couldn't dry my hands."

In 2005, with no tour to play on regularly, Brad took a job at Johnson & Wales to help his father run the golf program, which included not only coaching the team but also being in charge of the sixty students studying golf management. He did so with the proviso that he would get enough time off in the fall to go to the three stages of Q-School—if he made it to all three.

Adamonis started in early September and, inside of a week, his wife, Stacey, gave birth to the couple's first child. Four days after that, their world was turned upside down.

Dave Sr. had been diagnosed with prostate cancer, and went in for what was supposed to be routine surgery. Instead, something went terribly wrong. Urine started backing up into his body, which swelled terribly. His family was called to the hospital, and things were so dire that last rites were administered.

"As soon as I saw him in the hospital, I knew something was wrong," Brad says. "This guy never showed pain in his life. He tore an ACL once, and he walked off."

Emergency surgery saved Dave's life, but he came down with a staph infection and his weight plummeted from 210 pounds to 135.

He recovered from that, but the bad news kept on coming. When the prostate cancer was found, further screening revealed lymphoma. Upon checking out of his Florida hospital in December, with treatment at a Massachusetts hospital ahead, he was diagnosed with throat and tongue cancer too.

Brad spent most of his evenings that fall at Dave's hospital bedside, while his days were occupied with trying to keep the golf program on track at Johnson & Wales. His brother Dave came down to help out, but Brad says they were amazed at how many responsibilities the job entailed. "It was really a three- or four-person job, but he was a one-man show."

Finally, somebody else was hired to help. With all of this going on, Brad somehow gathered himself to make a bid at Q-School. Though he had hardly played any golf in preparation and had a lot weighing on his mind, he somehow managed to make it through the three stages and once again earn a Nationwide Tour card.

Dave Adamonis spent the first part of 2006 undergoing radiation treatments and chemotherapy while his son undertook his second run at the Nationwide Tour. But by that summer, Dave had recovered enough to come out and watch Brad at a couple of tournaments. One of those was in Scranton, Pennsylvania, where, inspired by his father's presence and resilience, Brad played so well that he was in the last group in the final round.

"To see him walking eighteen holes after all he'd been through was pretty amazing," Brad says. "I had some friends in the area who were watching, and Dad was out there walking ahead of everybody else. I figured if he could do that after all he had been through, I could win the tournament."

Brad almost pulled it off, missing a putt on the eighteenth hole that would have put him in a play-off.

The next year, he *did* win an event on the Nationwide Tour, the WNB Golf Classic in Odessa, Texas. He had to go through a marathon eight-hole play-off to finally get the victory. Meanwhile, his parents were back home trying to follow the play-off in real-time scoring on the PGA Tour's website, but unable to do so because the computer scoring system went down. After two hours of nearly unbearable suspense, they finally found out that Brad had won. Shortly thereafter, Brad called home. When his dad picked up the phone, Brad said, "Can you believe it?" His father's answer: "Yes, I can."

The victory wasn't enough to lift Adamonis into the top 25 on the Nationwide money list, so he didn't get a PGA Tour card that way. But he did finally break through the barrier at Q-School, where he finished ninth to finally get his ticket to golf's big time.

"It was great," says Adamonis about calling his father with the news. "After all the years of his sacrificing to help me out, I finally accomplished it. It should have happened a long time ago, but it did happen."

Dave Adamonis told a reporter late in 2007 that after suffering three forms of cancer, "there's no logical reason I'm still alive. I believe my will to stay alive is what saved me. I took the attitude that I still had things to do in life. I kept my mind occupied with all the things I need to do."

One of those things was his work at Johnson & Wales, which he returned to in the fall of 2006, a year after cancer struck. Now another of those things was to watch Brad play on the PGA Tour.

Dave was able to make it to the West Coast for a couple of events at the beginning of 2008, and before the AT&T Pebble Beach National Pro-Am he and Brad got to play Cypress Point, a gem that ranks as one of the top courses in the nation. It was a great experience, but Brad's caddie said that Dave looked tired, which proved to be an ominous sign.

When the tour came to Florida in March, Dave saw his son at the Honda Classic in Palm Beach Gardens, where he opened with a 76 but followed with a 66 to make the cut. The next week, Dave was unable to make the trip up to Tampa. His fight with throat cancer renewed, he headed again to Boston for treatments.

In June, Dave was able to watch Brad play the Travelers Championship in Connecticut, where he had his best finish so far: a tie for sixth. The next month, Brad bettered that showing, losing a play-off to Kenny Perry at the John Deere Classic in Illinois.

Then in August came awful news: Dave had lung cancer and part of his lung was removed. "It was bad luck for a guy who has given so much to other people," Brad says. "And he never even smoked."

Brad finished the year 124th on the money list, retaining his card for 2009 and earning a spot in the Players Championship in May. One week before the Players, Dave's doctors in Massachusetts did a biopsy and informed him that his lung cancer was now in an advanced stage.

But the terrible prognosis didn't keep Dave Adamonis down. The next week he traveled to Florida to watch Brad play in the Players Championship. He walked the first twelve holes of the first round before becoming short of breath and riding a cart the rest of the way.

Dave was an inspiration to all who saw him on that day, including Brad, who shot a 67. "It's a very special day," Dave told a reporter as Brad was signing his scorecard, his voice cracking with emotion. "It didn't make any difference what Brad shot. It was just special to be here."

As for his own plight, Dave said, "I'm going to treat it like every other challenge. I've never quit at anything in my life. I've always had a positive outlook on life. It's my makeup. We're going to go one day at a time, just like golf. You play a shot at a time; you take the good with the bad."

Dave battled to the end. He even returned to Johnson & Wales in September to try and get things in order there. When his condition took a turn for the worse, it was recommended that he enter a local hospice. Dave insisted that he wanted to return to New England for hospice care in his native Rhode Island, and that's where he spent his last ten days, finally succumbing to cancer in October.

"I lost my father and best friend, and it's tough. I used to talk to him every day, and I can't do that anymore. I really didn't want to play golf again for a while, to be honest," says Brad, who lost his PGA Tour card after 2009 and played the Nationwide Tour in 2010. "But it's something I still love to do, so I want to play well again and maybe do well for him too.

"I'm just proud that I had a father like my father. We had a lot of laughs. I'm proud and lucky too. I just hope I can be a father like that."

Stewart Cink

Courtesy of Stewart Cink

S tewart Cink is a major champion and six-time PGA Tour winner who has represented the United States in nine Ryder and
Presidents Cups. It's possible none of that would have happened if not for a decision his parents made when Stewart was a
toddler.

Neither Rob nor Anne Cink had ever played golf, but they decided to take up the game as a way to spend time together as a family and be outdoors. So, they headed out to Monrovia Golf Course, an inexpensive facility in their hometown of Huntsville, Alabama, and learned to play. Occasionally, Stewart would tag along and whack at balls with a left-handed six-iron.

A couple of years later, Rob was transferred to Florence, Alabama. The game had taken hold in the family, which by then also included a daughter, Danielle, and the Cinks joined Florence Country Club.

The small-town club, says Stewart "is not what most people think of when they think of a country club. It was a little golf course and a little clubhouse, very inexpensive."

It did have country club rules, though, and one of those rules was that children weren't allowed to play the course until they were eight years old. Until Stewart got old enough to go out on the course, Rob and Anne would leave him at the practice green while they played. In the summertime, Anne would take him to the club on a weekday and leave him for most of the day. There was no practice range, so it was strictly chipping and putting for young Stewart.

"I learned every inch of that putting green," Stewart says. "I wasn't alone; there were a couple of other kids like me. We would putt for a couple of hours, get a grilled cheese sandwich for lunch, and then go swim. Occasionally, we would go play in the woods, but someone would always come after us because they thought it was dangerous."

Stewart did sometimes sneak onto the course with his partner in crime—his father. On Mondays, when the course was closed, they would occasionally go out and play a six-hole loop. Stewart was so clearly into the game that it just didn't seem right to not let him play on the course at all.

When he turned eight, naturally, Cink was a demon around the greens.

"I didn't have much experience hitting the ball, but when I got around the green, I could get up and down," he says.

Now he could play golf with the same friends he used to hang around with on the putting green. "We would play thirty-six holes or more; we couldn't get enough. We were motivated to go out and try to beat each other, hit it farther, shoot our best score," he recalls. "We were always trying to improve."

By that time, Rob Cink had become a low-handicapper, not an easy feat for someone who took up the game as an adult—he got as low as a six-handicap. He wasn't schooled enough in the game to do much teaching to Stewart, but he did introduce him to the swing through Ben Hogan's book *The Five Fundamentals of Golf*. Florence Country Club pro Chris Burns also gave Stewart some pointers, but mostly he learned on his own.

"When parents ask me today about how much instruction to give their kids and how early to start, I say let the scorecard teach them," he says. "That's basically what I did until I was a teenager."

Considering his parents' motivation for learning the game, it was ironic that Stewart didn't get to play a lot of golf with them. Another club rule was partly to blame. Kids under the age of thirteen could not tee off before 3:00 PM on the weekend, and his parents generally played in their regular games early in the day.

"When I was eleven and twelve years old, I was shooting under par," Cink says, "and I still couldn't play until after three!"

Playing with Dad after school was out of the question because Rob came home too late. He had been transferred to Florence by the Georgia-Pacific lumber company, but then they closed down their Florence operation and Rob was out of a job. He ended up finding a place with a company that made doors, but it was an hour and a half away from home. The Cinks liked the schools where they were, and they liked the country club, so they decided to stay and have Rob make the long commute.

Still, the game served its purpose in bringing the family together. "I would pretty much go blow by blow in talking with my parents about my rounds. I knew they liked golf, so they were interested," Stewart remembers. "It was a big part of my relationship with my dad. It was a bond. He wasn't around that much, so I had to get attention any way I could."

Stewart's mom was the one who took an active role when he started playing junior tournaments, which came fairly early. She was the one who investigated what tournaments were available for Stewart to play in, and took him there.

"My first tournament was in Decatur [Alabama] when I was eight," Stewart says. "When I showed up, I noticed that there was one kid who was really upset. I asked my mom why, and she said, 'Before you came, he was the only one in his age group.' That kid ended up finishing second."

Cink played in a lot of Alabama Junior Golf Association tournaments when he was in the ten-and-under age division, and over the next several years kept stepping up the ladder in regional events.

"I was always moving into bigger ponds, where I was a smaller fish," Cink says. "I learned not to be intimidated by kids who had nice clothes and fancy golf bags."

Cink knows that his father would have liked to have gone to more tournaments, but he didn't have the type of job where he could take days off. He was able to impart some lessons along the way during the times they did get to play together. Two in particular stick in Stewart's mind to this day.

"He would never let me use a club that wasn't the right club. And if there was any doubt, he would make sure it was the club that would go over the green and not the one that would come up short," Stewart says.

Once, early on, when Stewart was young enough to still be using a junior set that had only a three-, five-, seven-, and nine-iron, they came to a par three of about 125 yards where Rob always had Stewart hit a three-iron.

"I remember *begging* him to let me hit a five-iron," Stewart says. "I was sure I could get a five-iron to that green. One day, he finally gave in. I remember I hit the most perfect five-iron I ever hit, and it came up five yards short. I remember thinking, 'He was right again!' It was so frustrating.

"I'm at a much more advanced level now, but I still never try to get too much out of a shot. There will be times when I think back to those days, and I'll think, 'There's no reason to try to muscle it.' There have been times that's been beneficial."

The other lesson came after the club built a practice tee — not a range, but an area from which you could hit shots into one of the fairways with your own shag balls.

"One time, we divided the shag balls in half. We each had about thirty balls. I hit all of mine before he got to his sixth or seventh ball," Stewart recalls. "He said, 'What are you in such a hurry for? You're never going to learn anything that way.' Now I take my time and make my practice shots count."

Another thing Cink picked up from his father was being meticulous about caring for his clubs, always cleaning dirt out of the grooves and keeping the grips clean and dry. "If Dad did it that way, I was going to," he said. "And I wanted to take care of what my parents gave me because I wasn't guaranteed to get another one. Besides, it helped with performance."

As much as he liked golf, soccer was actually Cink's favorite sport until he was fifteen. "I was a forward, I scored a lot, and I just loved it. But when I reported to practice when I was fifteen, I had put on weight, and the coach said, 'You're playing defense.'

"Well, that lasted one year, and that was it for soccer. I think what I liked about soccer was the showing-off part, scoring goals. In golf, I could show off on every shot."

At sixteen and seventeen, Cink was one of the top juniors in the nation. He couldn't afford to travel to California or the Northeast for tournaments, but he played around the Southeast. Most of his experiences were good, but Stewart remembers one in Tampa, Florida, that turned sour—and it happened to be at one of the few tournaments his father was able to travel to.

After a practice round, Stewart, then seventeen years old, went with some friends back to their hotel and was surprised to find they were traveling without their parents. What's more, they had beer in the room.

"I was a little scared. These guys were unsupervised and they were doing something totally against the rules," says Cink. "My buddy and I had a couple of beers and we left early. It turned out they did get rowdy and somebody busted the door."

That got the attention of the hotel, and, in turn, the American Junior Golf Association, which was running the tournament. The players involved named every kid who was there. Everyone, including Stewart, was disqualified before the tournament began for breaking the AJGA rules of conduct. And they were banned from the *next* tournament too. The whole family—Stewart's mother and sister had come along—had to make the ten-hour drive home together.

"I can't describe how bad I felt," says Stewart. "I tried to make excuses at first, but that was worthless. In a way, I was in the wrong place at the wrong time, but I did choose to go over there and I did choose to have a couple beers."

His parents didn't say much, basically giving him the silent treatment and letting him stew in his embarrassment. That wasn't typical of his father.

"He was pretty stern. He didn't tolerate any laziness or general irresponsibility. Even when we were little, if there were dirty clothes on the floor, we heard about it real quick," Stewart says. "He wasn't what you would call a 'players' coach' as a parent. His attitude was that he was working hard, so, by golly, everyone else had to work hard too. We had our moments around the house."

In golf, however, Stewart's father was as encouraging as anyone could possibly be. "Even shots I hit that were pretty poor, he would find a way to praise them," Stewart says.

Rob's attitude toward his own game was another matter. "He was always disgusted," says Stewart. "He's the most negative person about himself on the golf course that I've ever seen. Yet he was equally positive about the people he was playing with. That's something for psychologists, I guess.

"He would seem miserable all the way around the course. Then at the end of the round, he would say, 'That's one of the best days I've ever had on the golf course.' We would kid Dad about that."

While he was relentlessly positive about Stewart's game, Rob Cink considered himself a realist about his son's prospects of playing the PGA Tour, even as he moved through the top levels of junior golf.

"He had a good idea of what it would take, and I think he thought it was pretty unattainable for anybody," says Stewart. "It made me work harder to prove him wrong. He would say, 'Golf is great, but it's a one-in-a-million thing.' He was big about having something to fall back on."

In any case, it was golf that opened up Stewart's horizons, whether or not he made it as a pro. Without the game, the family wouldn't have had the financial resources to send Stewart to college anywhere except the University of North Alabama in their hometown. Instead, Cink had the pick of college scholarships (a 4.0 grade point average in high school didn't hurt either) and ended up going to Georgia Tech.

"'We can't afford that' were four words that were heard very often in our house," Stewart says. "Mom had to take a job, and I'm pretty sure they were living paycheck to paycheck. And my golf was one of the big reasons."

The investment paid off, but it wasn't part of a master plan.

"It just worked out that way," Stewart says. "Golf was a big thing for everyone in the family."

Cink graduated from Georgia Tech in 1995 with a degree in management. But he also had an idea that he wouldn't need his backup plan. He was named college Player of the Year as a senior — the same year that Tiger Woods was a freshman at Stanford.

Upon turning pro, Cink received a sponsor's exemption from the Canon Greater Hartford Open and got his career off to a fast start when he tied for eighteenth there and won $15,120.

"I was married by then, and we were dirt-poor," says Cink. "We had minus five hundred dollars in our checking account until I got a loan from [management company] IMG to pay some bills. Back then, you still had to wait to get the newspaper the next day to see how much you made. The fifteen thousand felt like a gazillion dollars. I called my parents, and it sounded like a gazillion dollars to them too."

Cink didn't earn a PGA Tour card at that winter's Qualifying School, but it didn't slow him down much. He won three times on the Nike Tour (now the Nationwide Tour) in 1996 to lead the money list and play his way onto the PGA Tour. Since then, he's finished outside the top 60 on the money list only once while collecting nearly $30 million in earnings.

These days, Stewart's parents make it to a couple of tournaments a year, but in his early years on the tour, they would come to eight to ten events a year and Rob would follow his son every step of the way. In fact, he would arrive at the range early enough to catch Stewart hitting all of his warm-up shots.

"I still don't know why; he's never told me," Stewart says. "I don't know if he just wanted to see all of my shots or if he wanted to see how I was swinging."

Not that Rob ever offered any advice on the swing or course management once Stewart hit the tour, realizing that his son was now on a higher level.

"He never had a lot to say about my performance," said Stewart. "If I played well, he would talk about it. If I played bad, he would just say, 'Go get 'em tomorrow.'"

It was similar to the approach Rob took all along.

"It was really smart, looking back," says Stewart. "With Dad's limited knowledge of the game, he gave me the right dose of teaching, which was a small dose. Other than that, he saw I had a real zeal for the game, and he let me go."

Ray Floyd

Courtesy of Ray Floyd

R aymond Floyd was so young when he hit his first golf ball that he can't even remember it. But he knows where it oc-curred—at his father's driving range.

L.B. Floyd was the pro at the Army course at Fort Bragg in North Carolina and he also owned a nearby range. It didn't take L.B., or anyone else, long to notice that his young son was a prodigy.

When Ray was five years old, crowds would gather at the range to watch him swat a golf ball farther than they thought possible for such a little tyke. Many years later, after his son had become a major champion, L.B. reflected back on those days for a *Sports Illustrated* writer. "I had to stop taking him there because the people would all stop and watch him hit. Nobody was buying any balls."

Looking back, Ray realizes that it was always L.B.'s dream for him to become a pro golfer. It remained unspoken, though, until Ray was in high school and expressed his desire to play professionally.

That desire materialized a few years earlier when L.B. took his eleven-year-old son to the Azalea Invitational, a PGA Tour event in Wilmington, North Carolina, ninety miles away. "I was so enthralled and excited I knew right then that was what I wanted to do," Ray remembers.

That was the first time Ray saw how the best players in the world did it, but as a member of the Floyd family of Fayetteville, he was already steeped in golf: his father was a pro; his mother, Edith, a club champion; and his little sister, Marlene, also took to the game and eventually became an LPGA Tour pro.

The patriarch of that golfing clan didn't play the game himself as a youngster. L.B. (his seldom-used given name was Loren Bethea) grew up in South Carolina with eight sisters and no brothers. He was only introduced to the game when he was in the Army, stationed at Fort Bragg in 1941. Even then, he played his first round as a reluctant favor to some buddies on the fort's baseball team who were looking for a fourth.

"I told them I didn't want to play cow-pasture pool," he later recalled.

L.B. was quickly hooked, though. And it became his life work when Marty Furgol, a tour pro who was stationed with him at Fort Bragg, told L.B. that, with his patience, he had the makings of a teaching pro.

He stayed in the Army as he pursued his golf calling to become the pro at Fort Bragg's Stryker Golf Course, the place he had learned to play. He rose to the rank of master sergeant, but didn't wear a uniform to work. Nor did he run his house like a drill sergeant.

"Dad was pretty laid-back," Ray says. "We were type B personalities, not Type As. But he did certainly have a way of making his point. He didn't say a lot, but when he did, you listened. He was subtle in his ways, but not an introvert by any means."

Naturally, Ray learned the golf swing from his dad. "He was big on fundamentals. He felt that if you had your fundamentals right, you could be a good player. He was the first person who had me lay a club down on the ground to make sure I was aimed properly."

Born in 1942, Ray grew up when junior sets of clubs were not as common as they are today, but, thanks to his dad, he was outfitted with a Byron Nelson MacGregor junior set that had a driver, a three-wood, five-, seven-, and nine-irons, and a putter. Ray started going out on the course when he was five. By the time he was thirteen, he was consistently shooting around par.

By then, he was already outscoring his father, whose play was limited by his multiple responsibilities at the course, which included maintenance supervisor as well as pro. L.B. did make time to play with his son, but that was not always a pleasant experience for Ray.

"He wanted me to be so precise that he was always giving me a lesson when we were playing. I didn't enjoy playing with him," says Ray. "That's one thing I learned that I applied when I was a father. When I went out with my boys [Raymond Jr. and Robert], I always said, 'Just enjoy it.' It was thrilling for me to have them say they wanted to play with me. I never gave them a lesson on the course, unless they asked about something. When we finished, I might tell them, 'This is why you were pull-hooking the ball today,' or something like that."

Even when Ray would get a good result with a shot, it wouldn't spare him from L.B.'s penetrating analysis. "The most important thing in the golf swing for him was balance," Ray says. "I could hit a ball perfect, but he'd say, 'That's no good. Your balance was bad.'"

In other ways, L.B. was more subtle. When Ray, who loved all sports, would get so involved with baseball or football that golf was shoved too much to the side, L.B. would tell him, "I'm going to sell your clubs if you're not going to play." That usually got Ray back on the course.

Courtesy of Ray Floyd

Those other sports gradually fell by the wayside; Ray quit football after ninth grade and basketball a year later. But he had a hard time letting go of baseball, where he was an outstanding pitcher. Through his junior year of high school, Ray played on both the baseball and golf teams even with their conflicting schedules. "I would pitch on either Tuesday or Friday, and play golf on the other," Floyd recalls.

But baseball was never part of the fabric of Ray's life as golf was. "I was always around the golf course. That was my life."

Not only did he play and practice, he also worked at the Fort Bragg course growing up, sometimes in the pro shop and sometimes on the maintenance crew. "I remember mowing fairways at age thirteen, making twenty-five cents an hour and loving it," he says.

Toward the end of his high school years, Ray worked even harder on a golf course. That's when L.B. retired from the Army, bought a nine-hole public course in Fayetteville, Green Valley Country Club, and expanded it to eighteen holes.

Between the extensive work on the existing nine and the construction of a new nine from scratch, there was plenty that needed to be done, and Ray pitched in as part of the family endeavor. "I was dragging, clearing, doing things of that nature," he recalls. "I didn't have the skills for shaping, but I did anything that could be done in a rough sense."

Ray finally quit baseball in his senior year after having been inspired by watching the Masters on television. But baseball wasn't quite through with him yet.

After he graduated, a major league scout for the Cleveland Indians convinced him to practice for a couple of weeks and get his arm loose for a tryout. He did, and the scout was impressed enough to offer him a $25,000 contract.

Still just seventeen years old, Floyd would have needed his father to cosign the contract.

"I asked Dad what he thought I should do, and he said, 'What do you want to do?'" Ray remembers. "I said, 'I really want to be a pro golfer, but that's a lot of money. Maybe I could try baseball for a couple of years and see if it works out.'

"Dad said, 'That's not right. If golf is what you really want to do, you would be cheating yourself and you would be cheating that man across the table if you sign this contract.'

"It was a lesson in integrity that I will always remember."

L.B. *did* want his son to get a college education, something no one on either side of the family had done. And golf afforded Ray that opportunity, as he earned a scholarship from the University of North Carolina.

Ray won the National Jaycees Junior tournament in the summer after high school and headed to Chapel Hill without the same enthusiasm for education his father had.

"I really didn't want to go to college," Ray admits. "I just wanted to play golf. At that time, everybody had to do two years in the Army. When I started at UNC, all I could see was four years of college, followed by two years in the Army, and I didn't want to wait that long to try the tour."

So, after one semester, Ray packed up his belongings, headed home, and told his mom and Dad that he was quitting school.

"Of course, he was heartbroken," Ray says of his father. "But we sat down and had a man-to-man talk. I told him that golf is my love and that's what I wanted to do. If it weren't for my love of golf, I would have signed that baseball contract."

Ray's plan called for going into the Army Reserve, which meant six months of active duty, followed by a limited commitment of two weeks or less at a time in ensuing years. As it turned out, his unit was called into active duty during the Cuban crisis. The call-up actually worked to Floyd's benefit, as he was able to complete his commitment in quick fashion. He served a year at Fort Bragg and then was released, free to pursue his professional golf dream.

Upon hitting the tour in 1963 at the age of twenty, Floyd became one of the youngest players ever to win a PGA Tour event when he captured the St. Petersburg Open that March. It was only the second cut he made, and the $3,500 first prize represented his first paycheck, since he finished out of the money the previous time he finished seventy-two holes.

Once he hit the tour, Ray would have a weekly chat with L.B. on the telephone. If there was anything in his swing that didn't feel right, Ray would ask his dad for a diagnosis. As it turned out, L.B.'s advice often worked.

Incidentally, Ray's swing as a young man was nothing like the idiosyncratic move he displayed later in his career.

"I had a beautiful swing early on," Ray says. "If you were to go back to film of me playing in those days, you would say, 'Holy cow, that's not Ray Floyd.' Later on, my golf swing started evolving around a bad back."

It was instructor Jack Grout—Jack Nicklaus's teacher—who helped Floyd find his new swing and turn his game around. When Floyd went to Grout in 1972, it was the first time he had ever seen another teacher besides his father.

"My swing had gotten very short and laid off because of my back," Floyd says. "Jack gave me that right-elbow move to get into the hitting position. My dad wasn't quite as sophisticated with teaching at the tour level. He knew I was laid off, but we weren't able to fix it. Neither of us had a problem with me going to another teacher."

Ray received another benefit from going to Grout. Unlike his dad, Grout would constantly pump him up. "He would tell me how great I was, that was the psychology," Floyd says. "He would give me a couple of pointers and when he finished, he would say, 'I don't know how anybody can beat you with the short game you have,' or something like that. I would come out of it feeling great."

It's not that L.B. didn't *think* his son was great. He just wasn't as steeped in the psychological aspect of the game, Ray believes.

Even after Ray began seeing Grout, he still would take lessons from his father when he was at a tournament near the Carolinas that L.B. could get to. L.B. was so strong on the fundamentals, and had such a good eye for the golf swing, that he could spot where Ray might have gotten off track.

Sometimes, Ray's dad would make corrections based on what he saw at a televised tournament, though that could be tricky because of the camera angles. But even without seeing Ray swing, L.B. could often solve the problem.

"I could tell him that I kept pulling a lot of shots or blocking a lot of shots, and he would say, 'Here's the first thing you do.' It was always back to the basics. It could be alignment, or not completing the backswing, or regripping. It would reinforce my fundamentals, and it's amazing how often there was something there."

That was the benefit of having a golf teacher for a father. And an excellent golf teacher, at that. Besides guiding Ray and Marlene to their respective tours, L.B. also tutored Fayetteville's Chip Beck, who became a fine tour player himself. L.B. said that his proudest day in golf came when Ray and Chip finished 1–2 in the 1986 US Open at Shinnecock Hills.

L.B. continued teaching lessons almost to his death in 2004 at the age of eighty-three. In his latter years, one of his students was a Fayetteville youngster named David Chung. In 2010, a twenty-year-old Chung was runner-up in the US Amateur.

"As far as I know, everybody who ever played golf around here took lessons from Daddy," Marlene says.

After her tour days, Marlene went on to run a golf-instruction school. When teaching women, who often don't generate enough clubhead speed, Marlene often imparts the same advice her dad gave her: "Swing at it hard in case you hit it."

Ray says that his father was an excellent teacher for the average golfer, perhaps even more so than for a tour-caliber player. He also was a major figure in public golf in Fayetteville. After buying and revitalizing Green Valley, L.B. sold it and built a new public course, Cypress Lakes, which opened in 1968.

"I love the game and I wanted to give the working man a chance to play golf and for their children to be able to get started," L.B. once told the *Fayetteville Observer*.

For those and other efforts, L.B. Floyd was inducted into the Carolinas Golf Hall of Fame in 1997. He got there on his own, but he also played a role in raising a World Golf Hall of Famer in Ray, who finished with twenty-two victories on the PGA Tour, including four major championships.

One of those came in 1976 at the Masters in Georgia. That's the tournament L.B. had attended many years before and dreamed that his son would one day play there. It was also the tournament that inspired Ray when he watched on television in 1959 and solidified his desire to become a pro golfer.

When the final putt fell to wrap up Ray's victory in 1976, L.B. turned to a friend and said, "This is what a father always dreams of."

Bill Haas

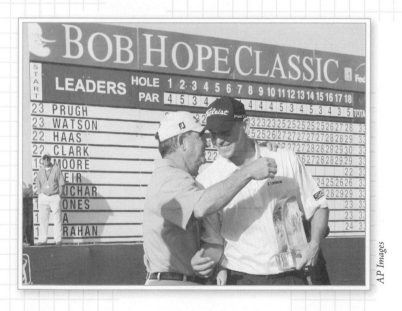

L ittle kids usually don't fully appreciate what their father does for a living, and that was true for Bill Haas about his dad, PGA Tour professional Jay Haas.

"I realized that he played golf for his job. But it wasn't probably until I was ten or eleven that I realized how good he was and that he was one of the few able to do that job," says Bill, now a pro himself and a two-time winner on the PGA Tour in 2010. "Until then, I kind of figured that anybody could do it if they wanted."

Bill actually grew up wanting to be an NBA player. At about the same time he realized how special his dad was at golf, he also figured out that a pro basketball career probably wasn't in the cards for him. But it was only much later—not until his second year of college—that Bill thought he could follow his dad's footsteps onto the PGA Tour.

"When I was in high school, I never really expected to get on the PGA Tour because I knew how good they were," Bill says. "I was very realistic in knowing how hard it was."

It was only natural that Bill would play golf from an early age. Even before he started playing, Bill recalls that he and his brother, Jay Jr., would put on baseball gloves and catch Jay's shots on the range. But he doesn't remember much about his early days on the golf course because he didn't take the game all that seriously until his middle school years.

For his part, Jay was very careful not to impose the game on Bill, or any of his five children (two boys and three girls). "He was never the type to say, 'Bill, we have to go to the range to work on your game.' He didn't want to push me into it. He was glad to give me advice, but only if I asked."

With so many kids in the family, and tour-provided day care not being what it is today, the Haas children didn't travel on the PGA Tour very much. "The only tournaments we went to were fun ones. We would go to Disney every year," Bill says. "And the Masters was a big one. That was close to home, so we could drive to it."

While having a tour pro for a father meant that Dad was away from home a lot, there were compensating factors. For one thing, when Jay was taking time off from the tour, it meant he was home all day, every day. That meant plenty of opportunities for Bill to play golf, or do other things, with Dad. For another, it meant getting to know the PGA Tour players who were his father's buddies.

Jay hosted a charity pro-am at his home course in Greenville, South Carolina, every year that featured some top pros. "It was nice knowing they were regular people who happened to be good at golf," Bill says.

Jay was particularly good friends with former Wake Forest teammate Curtis Strange, so Bill got to know him well. Fred Couples, another friend, once came to spend two weeks at the Haas house when Bill was young. Bill also had two uncles who played on the tour, his dad's brother Jerry Haas and his mom's brother Dillard Pruitt, as well as a great-uncle who won the 1968 Masters, Bob Goalby.

Watching his family and the other pros swing helped influence how Bill played the game. "Dad never said that his way was the only way to do it. He would tell me to watch other players. If I saw something I liked in Fred Couples's swing, I could try to emulate him."

Bill's game developed from a combination of small tips from his father, watching other pros, and figuring things out on his own. It wasn't technically oriented.

"I never thought about trying to get to a certain position at the top of the swing. I never looked at a video," Bill says. "It's a home-grown swing, not a manufactured one."

And most of the learning happened on the golf course, not the driving range.

"Something Dad stressed to me was that you're going to have certain shots on the course that you're never going to hit on the range," Bill says. "I would get in thirty-six holes pretty often, and I didn't spend a lot of time on the range. Even today, I don't go to the range much. I warm up before I play. Then, if I play well, I think why should I go to the range and mess it up."

Bill developed a swing that is not very much like his dad's and also a different kind of game. While Jay's strength is accuracy, Bill is a long hitter.

"A lot of that is the arc of your swing. I'm six foot two and he's five ten or five eleven. That enabled me to have a bigger arc," says Bill. "I was lucky that way."

Bill's thirty-six-hole days started when he was about twelve years old, after the family moved from the town of Travelers Rest north of Greenville to a home at a new course nearby that Jay was involved in, the Thornblade Club. Bill's interest in the game was burgeoning at that time. It was encouraged by pro Jamie McCullough and the welcoming atmosphere for juniors at the club.

Bill made the high school team when he was in seventh grade, though he readily admits that the team wasn't very good and he was shooting about 45 for nine holes at the time. When he was thirteen and fourteen, Bill was shooting around 80 for eighteen, but in his freshman year of high school, he suddenly improved to shooting between par and 75.

Even then, golf was still mostly a summer pursuit. Bill continued to play basketball through his junior year of high school, though he didn't advance past the junior varsity. He played in junior golf tournaments during the summer, but mostly around South Carolina and only a limited number of national events.

The one thing that Bill had his eye on in those years was a college scholarship. His uncle Jerry had moved from the PGA Tour to being the golf coach at Wake Forest, where both he and Jay had played. "My motivation was to get good enough to earn a scholarship, and not just because my uncle was the coach," says Bill.

Bill managed to beat his father only once when he was in high school. Just doing it once was an impressive feat, considering that his dad was a top 60 player on the PGA Tour at the time.

It happened on a chilly New Year's Day in 1999 at a South Carolina course called The Cliffs at Keowee Vineyards.

"We weren't really keeping score on the scorecard," Bill recalls, "but when we got to the seventeenth tee, he said, 'Bill, you're beating me by two shots.' I said, 'I know.' I parred the last two holes and beat him by one or two with a 69 to his 70 or 71.

"I told him it didn't really count. When it happened, I wanted it to be where I shot 64 and he shot 65 or something like that. But he said, 'It counts. I was trying on every shot.'"

Bill didn't manage to beat Dad very often when he was in college either, even though he was one of the top amateurs in the country by the time he graduated. In truth, they didn't get a chance to play together very much in those years, with Bill playing a busy amateur schedule in the summer in addition to being away at school the rest of the year and Jay continuing to play the tour. They did stay in frequent contact by telephone.

"He was very involved, but he never called and said, 'You shot 75, you have to work on it.' It was quite the opposite. He would ask me what I was doing well," Bill says. "He was still my main teacher. When I was lost, I would call my dad and say, 'I'm hooking it.' And he would give me a tip."

Bill also benefited from his uncle Jerry coaching the Wake Forest team. "He was the coach, but he was the best player on our team. Jerry was always there, so he was more hands-on."

After a freshman year that was pretty good but did not include any individual victories, Bill stepped his game up to another level. "Before that, I didn't think I had a chance to play on the tour. Then I started beating some of the guys who were good enough that they thought they would be playing the tour. I began to feel that I could play out there."

In the summer after his sophomore year, Haas was medalist at the 2002 US Amateur and advanced to the semifinals of match play.

He followed that by earning first-team All-America honors for the second straight year as a junior at Wake Forest.

Haas had been attending summer school in order to assure graduation in four years while playing a rigorous college golf schedule. Now figuring that his future likely lay on the PGA Tour, he didn't want to go to summer school after his junior year.

"I talked it over with my dad and he said it was my decision but that I would have to talk to my mom [Jan] first. She said, 'No, you're graduating.' My mom usually has the last say, and she's usually right."

After attending summer school, Bill reached the quarterfinals of the US Amateur and was named to the United States Walker Cup team for the competition against Great Britain and Ireland. Then he not only garnered first-team All-American honors for the third straight year as a senior, he also was named Player of the Year and finished second in the NCAA Championship. His last event as an amateur was the 2004 US Open, where he and Jay both competed for the second straight year. Both had missed the cut in 2003, but this time Bill finished tied for fortieth and Jay tied for ninth. The only other father-and-son duo to play in the same US Open was Joe Kirkwood Sr. and Jr. in 1948.

Jay joined the PGA Tour in 1977 and was a nine-time winner on that circuit over the course of a career marked by consistency and longevity. He staged a renaissance at the age of forty-nine in 2003, convincing him to play mostly on the regular tour in 2004 and 2005 instead of joining the Champions Tour for players over fifty. That afforded Jay and Bill the chance to play in seventeen tournaments together. Bill managed to beat his dad on only five of those occasions.

"To this day, even at fifty-seven years old, he's still really good," Bill says. When they play casual rounds, "We'll joke around and have fun, but we're also working on our games. We always putt everything out and when it comes to the eighteenth, we know what we're shooting. When it comes down to it, I want to beat him. When I do, it's satisfying, just because he is so good."

The first time they played in the same PGA Tour event was in Greensboro in 2002 when Bill got a sponsor's exemption as an amateur. After Bill turned pro in June 2004, he received exemptions into eight tournaments that year as a result of his amateur achievements and attempted to earn a PGA Tour card without going to Q-School. Meanwhile, Jay qualified for the US Ryder Cup team that played at Oakland Hills, where Bill was on hand to watch. Bill had also gone to South Africa in 2003 when Jay played in the Presidents Cup.

"Some of my best memories of watching him play are from that Presidents Cup and Ryder Cup," Bill says.

Bill also gained some great memories from playing with his father in a couple of team competitions in 2004, winning the CVS Charity Classic and finishing fourth in the Franklin Templeton Shootout, a couple of unofficial PGA Tour events.

Bill fell short of getting a tour card via his earnings in 2004, and his performance at that fall's Q-School ended up earning him status only on the Nationwide Tour. But he did gain entry into six PGA Tour events in 2005, and his father joined him in the field for every one of them.

"I wish I could have gotten onto the tour sooner, so we could have played a whole season together," Bill laments. "That would have been fun."

Bill made it through Q-School to join the tour in 2006. By then, Jay had turned most of his attention to the Champions Tour, but he did play in four events with his son that year. In the last of those, Bill finished tied for fourth at the Wachovia Championship. That was practically the high-water mark of a somewhat frustrating first three years on the PGA Tour, when he finished between 99th and 104th on the money list.

It was a rocky start to a tour career for a player given the "can't miss" label, not to mention one who was following in the large footsteps of his father. Jay counseled his son to be patient. "He would tell me that the one thing he couldn't teach me was experience — that I would have to learn myself. It's hard to be patient at a young age. I wanted to do well early. But, he would say that golf's a marathon, not a sprint," Bill says.

Things got a little better in 2009 when Bill moved up to sixty-first on the money list, and the breakthrough came in 2010 with two victories and a ranking of twentieth on the list with earnings of nearly $3 million. Bill's first victory, at the Bob Hope Classic in California, was a great moment for the Haas family as Jay was able to be on hand, thanks to a Monday finish because of a rare rained-out day in the desert.

Actually, the family doings started the previous Monday. Jay was in the California desert at his teacher Billy Harmon's home course to work on his game before heading to Hawaii that week to play a Champions Tour event. Jay Jr. and Jay's uncle Bob Goalby were also on hand. Bill was able to join them only because he missed the cut the previous week at the Sony Open in Hawaii.

Frustrated with his play at that event, Bill got a simple tip from Harmon about turning his right foot out at address. That tip turned his game around and put him in contention at the Hope. With Bill one stroke out of the lead entering the final round, Jay sent him a text message Sunday night that read, "Hit when you're ready, and never before." Then Jay hopped on a red-eye from Hawaii to be on hand for the Hope final round, which he watched from behind the ropes. It was the first time Jay had a chance to watch Bill at a tournament in two years.

Bill was so focused, and Jay so unobtrusive, that he never saw his dad that day until after he had won — his birdie on the eighteenth hole was followed by a warm hug from Jay. Making it even better was that Bill's name was joining his father's on the Bob Hope trophy; Jay won the event in 1988.

While their time together is limited mostly to the off-season these days, Bill remains in constant touch with his father. "I talk to him or text him after just about every round," Bill says. "He's played almost every course I'm playing; he can relate to everything I'm doing. There's no better person to go to for advice."

Bill has found only one difficulty in following his father onto the PGA Tour. Jay not only set the bar high with his nine victories, he set it even higher by being one of the nicest and classiest guys on the tour.

"The hardest part of trying to learn and to be like him is how to handle yourself off the golf course. In five years on tour, I've yet to find anyone who said, 'Your dad's a jerk,'" says Bill, who, it should be noted, is a nice guy himself. "I always have people coming up and telling me how nice a guy my dad is, and how professional he is. I would like to be half that."

J.J. Henry

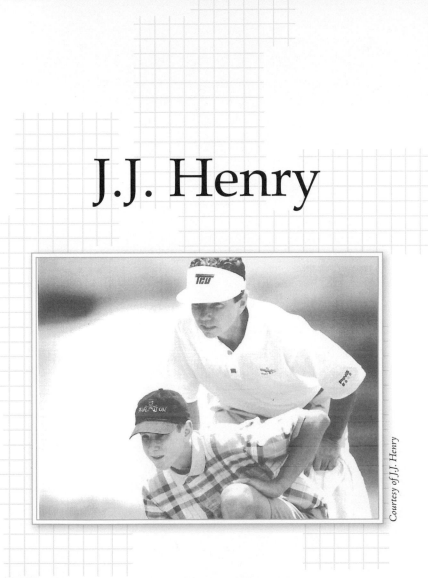

J.J. Henry is proud to be Ronald J. Henry III, even if it isn't the name he goes by. The pride lies in carrying the mantle of the father and grandfather who have been so influential in his life, both inside and outside of golf.

The first Ronald J. Henry started a real estate company in Fairfield, Connecticut, in 1937 that is still going strong today, now guided by Ronald J. Henry Jr. When J.J. was growing up, his father and grandfather were both members of the Patterson Club in Fairfield, affording the youngster a place to play and practice.

J.J. was introduced to the game at a putting green and bunker in his grandfather's backyard. Another early field of play was the beach, which was right behind his parents' house. As early as five or six years old, J.J. would go out and whack a golf ball from jetty to jetty, where in ensuing years he would be joined by his younger brother Kevin and often by their dad.

(Ronald J. Jr., by the way, was known as Jay to his friends from his middle initial, which stands for Joseph. Ronald J. III became known as Jay Jr., which got abbreviated as J.J. "That's what everybody has always called me," says J.J. "On the first day of school, the teacher would call me Ronald and I would raise my hand and say that I'm J.J.")

J.J. did not limit himself to golf when he was growing up, nor did his parents push him toward the course, though his father was a top-notch amateur player who was a regular at the Connecticut State Amateur and who eventually would go on to play a number of times in the US Amateur, US Mid-Amateur, and British Amateur. J.J. played soccer, basketball, baseball, lacrosse, tennis, and was on swimming teams. "The only sport I never played was football," he says.

Ultimately, J.J. zeroed in on two sports. One was basketball, where Henry, who grew to be six foot three, went on to play shooting guard for one of the top high school teams in the state. The other was golf, which he began to take more seriously when he was nine or ten years old.

Henry wasn't a golfing wunderkind, but he made steady progress. He recalls that he first broke 80 when he was twelve or thirteen years old. Arriving at the eighteenth hole needing a par to shoot in the 70s, he stroked a four-wood that rolled to within four feet of the hole for a birdie putt that gave him a 78.

Within a year, he beat his father for the first time. That was no mean feat, considering that his father was a scratch player. But he didn't go to his father for swing instruction.

"I wouldn't say my dad was the best ball striker," says J.J. "He was a great chipper and putter, and that's what enabled him to score. I did learn a lot about course management and the mental side of things from him, and competitiveness. I also learned to enjoy myself. The big thing about my dad was that he always wanted to make sure we were having fun."

While Ron Henry Jr. knew enough about his son's swing to be able to watch him hit balls and give him a couple of tips, most of J.J.'s early instruction came from Patterson pro Paul Kelly. It involved more than lessons on the range.

"Paul Kelly loved playing golf. When they would close up the pro shop at five, or six, or seven o'clock, I would say, 'All right, pro, we are going to go out,' and we would play until dark. Sometimes we would play a cross-country game," J.J. remembers.

"Golf was always fun for me. With some parents, it's very regimented. They'll say, 'I want you to putt for an hour and hit balls for an hour and then I'll be here to pick you up.' That's not the way it was."

J.J. gained another reason to spend time at the club when he became a caddie at around the age of twelve. It was a way to connect even more to the game, learning about its rituals, traditions, and level of sportsmanship, and also a chance to make some extra money.

He would sometimes caddie in his father's group. But as he moved into high school, he increasingly would join as a player. In either role, J.J. learned a lot. "I saw my dad's and his friends' demeanor on the golf course. I learned to respect the guys you're playing with," he says. "By being around the game, I picked up on the honesty and integrity that go along with it. It was also about having a good time."

The group of regulars was made up of low-handicap amateurs who liked betting action when they played, and J.J. joined right in. "If I played well, I could win twenty or thirty dollars, which was nice when you're a freshman in high school," Henry remembers.

But his father generally wouldn't cover his losses. "I had to make sure I had enough money to cover it," says J.J. "That's why he wanted me to have money from caddying. Sometimes when the other guys wanted me to play, Dad would say, 'No, he needs to caddie. He needs to make money.' And they would say, 'No, we need him to play.'"

Caddying played a big role in the Henrys' relationship. In his early teen years, J.J. toted the bag for his father at the Connecticut State Amateur; when J.J. was nineteen years old, he *won* the state amateur with his father on his bag.

"My dad unfortunately never got a chance to win one of those big events," J.J. says. "When I won the Connecticut State Amateur, it felt like I won the US Open. After I caddied for him, it was really neat for it to come full circle and have him caddying for me when I won. My dad had tears in his eyes, as did I. You go through a lot of highs and lows playing in a match play event, and it was great to be together with your dad through all of that."

Later, J.J. gave his dad a Father's Day present—two photographs, one showing J.J. caddying for him at the Connecticut State Amateur and the other showing J.J. lifting the trophy after he won.

There were times in Henry's high school years when the two competed in the same tournament. "I wanted to kick his butt," J.J. admits. "I was always asking him, 'Dad, what did you shoot?'"

Ron Jr. was an accomplished-enough player to win the Patterson Club championship six times. J.J. didn't play in the club championship for very many years, but he won it once—and scored a victory over his father in the semifinals.

"It was fun," J.J. says. "I'm not sure who my mom was rooting for—probably my dad."

J.J.'s junior career began in the Borck Memorial, a big local tournament in Fairfield, when he was twelve years old. "Dad gave me some advice going in," he says. "One thing I remember is that he said never to slam your driver after a bad shot. It shows weakness to your fellow competitors. When you're twelve, it's good to have somebody who understands and can help you."

J.J.'s mother, Nancy, was usually the one who took him to junior tournaments, but his father's schedule was flexible enough that he was able to be there sometimes too. The family's upper-middle-class standing helped them fund Henry's junior play, but he also appreciates that he wasn't handed everything.

"There were days when Dad said, 'You know what? You're caddying.' Even though Dad was successful in business, he didn't give me everything, and I think that's important," J.J. says. "Hopefully, I've learned that. You try to instill in kids how lucky you are, and how you have to work for certain things."

Henry won some state events and never lost a match in high school, but he wasn't a blue-chip recruit. He had a hard time getting into the more prestigious American Junior Golf Association events, which were invitationals, but managed to make the field for one in Arizona where college coaches were checking out prospects.

Oklahoma State coach Mike Holder and Texas Christian coach Bill Montigel watched him on the range, and both were wondering who this kid was and how they had missed him. Holder had already used up his scholarships, though, and that's how Montigel got Henry to TCU in Fort Worth.

"I always felt I was a player who was continuing to get better and better, even though I wasn't winning the US Junior or anything like that," says Henry. "I wasn't the can't-miss kid, but I knew I was good. I believed in myself, and I knew my dad and mom believed in me."

J.J.'s anticipation level for college golf had reached a fever pitch the summer after his junior year of high school when Ron qualified for his second US Amateur in 1992 (he also made it in 1988). J.J. caddied for his dad at Muirfield Village, and was inspired by seeing all the top college players in the field.

"I remember seeing all of the colors of the college teams and recognizing the players, and thinking how cool it would be to be one of those guys carrying the stand bags and playing," he says. "And I was learning a lot from being inside the ropes at such a big tournament."

J.J. got off to a slow start at TCU, a program that was well stocked with strong upperclassmen when he got there, seldom making the five-man playing squad for tournaments in his freshman year.

"I was frustrated," he says. "But I would talk to my dad on the phone, and he would remind me that if I was a freshman at a top basketball program, I probably wouldn't play much. He said that if I played in a tournament or two, that would be great."

The following summer, J.J. won the first of three Connecticut State Amateur titles, and he was on his way.

After graduating from TCU in 1998, Henry was given a sponsor's exemption to play in his home state's PGA Tour event, the Canon Greater Hartford Open, as an amateur. It was a thrill for both father and son, as J.J. shot a first-round 68 and made the cut. Soon after, he turned pro.

J.J. and his dad then embarked on a great adventure, where they formed a caddie-player team at the PGA Tour's Qualifying School. Q-School can be a nerve-wracking event, but having his dad along made it less so.

"I was right out of college, so it didn't feel like life or death at that point," J.J. says. "Q-School can be an ordeal, but I just thought it was cool. To be able to spend three weeks with my dad, enjoying a game that we had enjoyed since I was young and we were hitting balls back and forth on the beach was probably one of the best experiences I've ever had in my life."

Q-School consists of three stages, and Henry easily passed the first stage by finishing in the top 5 in Wilmington, North Carolina. The next stage was three weeks later at Houston's Deerwood Country Club.

Again concentrating on having fun with his dad, Henry played just well enough to make it into a play-off for the last spots. With ten players vying for eight spots in the Q-School finals, Henry parred the first play-off hole and he was in.

"We gave each other a hug, and said off we go in another month to Palm Springs," J.J. says. "We made a vacation out of it again." Henry remembers making a 7 on the first hole of the fourth round in the six-round final stage. "I was beside myself, feeling like I had blown it. Dad calmed me down, telling me it was a marathon, not a sprint."

Henry ended up missing a PGA Tour card by three strokes, but the news wasn't all bad news as his performance got him a full exemption on the secondary Nike Tour (now Nationwide Tour), which would prove to be his route to the main tour.

"It was really cool to have my dad there with me," says Henry. "We both felt he would be extremely helpful to me, and sure enough he was. Q-School has never kept a really good player from making the tour, but it can delay them. If not for my dad, I might not have made it the first time. He was extremely proud of what I accomplished."

It was the last time Henry's father caddied for him. As great an experience as it was, Ron II returned to his regular work confident that J.J. could make it on his own.

Henry has a vivid memory of pulling out of his parents' driveway at the end of 1998 in a Ford Expedition packed to the gills, driving to Florida to get ready for the Nike Tour.

"I remember them waving at me. It was like, 'Son, we're proud of you. We're glad we were able to help you reach your goal. Now, go out and do it.' It was like leaving the nest to go into the real world. And I was lucky enough that for me the real world was professional golf."

In his second year on the Nike Tour, Henry won a tournament and finished thirteenth on the money list to earn a PGA Tour card for 2000. Henry finished in the top 50 as a rookie on the big tour, a fine showing, but only after a slow start.

"After missing a cut, Dad would always say something positive to me when I talked to him on the phone," J.J. recalls. "He would say, 'Look at the guys you beat,' because there were always some good players who finished behind me. He wouldn't call and say, 'What happened? Why did you shoot 74?'

"He was always like that when I was growing up too. A lot of times in junior golf, you see parents who say, 'Why did you miss six greens?' or 'Why did you three-putt that hole?' But my dad understood from playing competitive golf himself. He was always trying to pick me up, he never beat me down."

J.J.'s parents were on hand when he scored his lone PGA Tour victory, which came at Hartford in 2006. And they made the trip to Ireland that year to watch J.J. play in the Ryder Cup after he qualified for the United States team.

"It was really great to have my dad at the Ryder Cup, because he was such a huge part in my getting there," says J.J. "Some of the best memories of my life are the ones I've experienced with my dad on the golf course."

Peter Jacobsen

E rling Jacobsen was all about doing things the right way. Especially golf.

The Jacobsens were very much a golfing family, but the kids didn't get an early start in playing the game. Before they became golfers, they learned the game as caddies at their dad's club,

Waverley Country Club in Portland, Oregon, beginning at twelve years old.

"Dad was adamant about learning the game through caddying first," says Peter, who grew up to be a seven-time winner on the PGA Tour and a US Senior Open champion. "That's how we were indoctrinated into the game. We learned the rules, we learned the etiquette, we learned to respect the game."

After a year as a caddie, Peter started playing regularly at the age of thirteen. The lessons about respecting the game continued as he played with his father, sometimes with one or more of his siblings (two brothers and a sister) and sometimes with other club members.

"Dad was a real stickler for the rules. He had a reverence for the game," says Peter. "We were schooled in etiquette the entire time we were on the golf course."

Erling was meticulous about replacing divots, making sure they fit into the divot hole like a piece of a jigsaw puzzle. He would replace other divots that he found on the course too, not just his own.

When the Jacobsen kids didn't respect the game, there were consequences, as Peter learned one day when he was thirteen or fourteen playing in a family foursome at Astoria Golf and Country Club on the Oregon coast. "I remember it like it was yesterday," says Peter. "We were on the third tee, I hit a bad drive, and I slammed my driver down so deep in the ground that it looked like a horse had made a mark on the tee.

"Dad took my bag and said, 'Peter, if you can't play properly, you're not going to play. Go to the car.' He told me to stand next to the car and not move. I stayed there while they played the rest of the round. It was a great lesson to me. It was a lesson on just how much he respected the game and expected others, including boys, to respect it and not act like a fool."

You can bet that Peter never slammed a club into the ground again.

Lapses such as that were the exception, as Peter not only took to the game itself but also the atmosphere and the unique opportunity to interact with his elders.

"We would play not just with Dad, but also with his friends at the club. You might be playing with somebody who was seventy, somebody who was forty. It helped me a great deal," says Peter.

"As a fifteen- or sixteen-year-old, you don't get the opportunity to hang out with adults much. Dad always encouraged us to talk to his friends and ask questions. I learned so much from people on the golf course when I was a teenager. It was fascinating for me. Unfortunately, it's something that is lost with so many restrictions on junior play at clubs today."

Erling's best friend at the club was a man named Bill Knight. Peter and one of his brothers would often either caddie in their foursome or fill out a foursome themselves as players.

"Bill had a son who had run track at the University of Oregon," Peter says. "He was so frustrated with his son because he didn't like golf. All he did was make shoes and try to sell them at track meets. I remember him saying that he was afraid his son wasn't going to make it."

Bill Knight's son, Phil, ended up making it after all, starting a company named Nike that has done pretty well.

Peter spent a lot of time at the course, caddying or playing, often both in the same day. He and his brother David, older by a year, would frequently take a bus to Waverley on summer mornings and be picked up at the end of the day by their dad. Even the Jacobsen property afforded opportunities to work on their game. The family built a putting green in the backyard, with Erling and David doing most of the work, and had regular family putting tournaments.

Their primary teacher was their father, who was a scratch player before the kids came along. It's said in the family that after David was born, Erling became a one-handicapper, and when Peter came along he became a two. Then came Susie and Paul, as Erling slipped to a four-handicap. But he knew the golf swing.

"He wasn't a teaching pro, but he was a real student of the game," says Peter. "He learned from some local players and a local teacher, and he passed that on to us."

And to others too.

"If you were to talk to people who knew my father, they would say he was addicted to the game," says Peter. "He would play in the morning, then he would go to the range and not only help us but he would walk up and down and help everyone else too. To this day, when I run into someone who knew my father or was a junior player in Portland, invariably they will come up and say, 'Your dad taught me.'"

Peter says that while his father had a "picture-perfect swing, better than mine," he was a very flexible teacher.

"People are going to swing the way they are going to swing. He was great at letting us play our own way," says Peter.

Erling also encouraged his children to copy the great players they saw on television, particularly on made-for-TV matches like the CBS Golf Classic and Shell's Wonderful World of Golf where they could watch their swings.

"Dad said if you want to hit a hook, swing like Arnold Palmer. If you want to hit a fade, swing like Lee Trevino. And Dad showed me how to do it. That's how I learned to impart spin on the ball."

Peter took emulating the pros to another level. He worked on imitations of various players' swings in the backyard to amuse the rest of the family. Those imitations, combined with his humor and effervescent personality, later made him a hit at tour practice ranges and clinics.

The three oldest Jacobsen children all played competitively, David and Susie at a high level as amateurs and Peter taking it all the way to the PGA Tour. All three got involved in competitive junior golf, but this aspect of the Jacobsen kids' makeup didn't come from their dad.

"He didn't like the competitive arena, tournament golf, me against you," says Peter. "He didn't get into gambling games. He just liked to play the game, talk about the swing, the golf course, the family, the game of golf. There were no Nassaus, no five dollars on the line. It was just enjoying the game, enjoying family and friends."

Once he saw the kids' interest level in junior golf, Erling was supportive, but from a distance. He paid the entry fees, but almost never went out and watched them play.

"It was because he got so nervous. I can understand that," Peter says.

One time Erling broke down and decided to watch Peter in the state high school championship as a senior, a tournament he ended up winning. After taking off from his work as an insurance salesman, Erling watched Peter play one hole.

"I made a bogey, he turned around, went back to the car, and told himself he was a jinx," says Peter, who didn't know his dad had come to watch him that day. "He didn't tell me about it until four years later."

Erling's disinclination for competition and his views on the importance of education are revealed by an anecdote from Peter's college years at the University of Oregon. Peter had taken some time off from the campus to come home and play in the Northwest Amateur. With one round to go, Peter told his dad that he was in second place in the tournament. "If you're going to waste your time in these tournaments and not win, maybe you should just go back to school and study," Erling harrumphed.

Peter didn't end up winning that tournament, but he did win the Oregon Amateur during his college years. Four years of college left him about a semester short of earning enough credits for graduation. He didn't have the money to go back and finish, and he had played well enough on the collegiate level to convince himself that he was ready to turn pro. At about the same time, he reached another decision. Peter had been dating Jan Davis, a player on the university's women's golf team, and decided to ask her to marry him.

"I gave Mom and Dad two bombshells at the same time—that I was quitting school to turn pro and going to marry Jan. They just about freaked out. I remember they said, 'No, you're not!'"

Nonetheless, Jacobsen turned pro that summer of 1976 and won the Northern California Open, his first event, collecting a big cardboard check that he still has and cashing a real one for $3,500. He played the minitours that summer, sailed through PGA Tour Qualifying School on his first try in December, and got married at the end of the month.

"Even at the wedding, friends of my mom and dad would come up to me and say, 'You know, you don't have to do this,'" Peter says. It wasn't that his parents, or their friends, didn't like Jan, but they thought it was too soon—and when he got his tour card, they figured it would be easier going on the road if he was single.

More than three decades later, Peter and Jan are still married, with three grown children of their own. "As I look back, it was the best decision I ever made," he says.

Turning pro worked out nicely too. The first year was a little bit rough, but Jacobsen settled in after that and remained a PGA Tour regular for twenty-seven years, winning more than $7 million.

Erling quickly warmed to the idea of Peter playing the tour, but rarely went to a tournament to watch him play in the early years. He did remain Peter's main confidante on the swing and other matters.

"I talked to him all the time. I always thought of him as my mentor. He was the last say for me on my golf game," Peter says. "When I was home, I would be out there playing with my father on Saturdays and Sundays."

One thing that changed for Peter on tour was that he began to wear a glove when he played. "We didn't wear gloves growing up because my father said that was an unnecessary expense," Peter says. "I only used a glove on tour because the equipment reps would put them in my locker. I figured if it's free, I might was well use it."

The Jacobsen family's world was rocked in 1984 by the news that Erling had throat cancer. After an operation, it was very difficult for him to talk and to be understood, but it didn't diminish his spirit for life or his love of golf. He continued to walk up and down the range at Waverley, helping people with their games. And he began to get out on the PGA Tour more with Peter, who wanted to spend as much time as possible with his dad.

Erling, by now a ten-handicapper, played in some pro-ams and enjoyed getting to know some tour players, many of whom made the effort to get to know him. "It warmed my heart the way my friends on the tour embraced my dad," says Peter. "We're like a big family out there."

Erling's last competitive round was at the 1992 Los Angeles Open pro-am, with actor Jack Lemmon. Later that year, cancer took his life. Before that happened, Peter had a chance to put a club in his dad's hands so he could waggle it.

"What's the most important thing in golf, Dad?" Peter asked.

"Sense of humor," Erling replied.

That's a lesson Peter had taken to heart long before as one of the PGA Tour players who best understands the entertainment aspect of professional golf.

It's one of many lessons Peter learned from his dad. "I can't stress enough how important my dad was in my life and in my development as a player," he says. "He taught me right from wrong on the golf course and in life."

While his father was tough and strict, Peter said that didn't lead to tension or to any rebellion on his part.

"No, there was none of that. I loved my father so much, and I respected him. He wasn't mean, he wasn't cruel. We had a voice in things and we had a lot of fun, but we had to do things the right way. I respected his rules because he was my father and he knew better. And now I respect him more than ever."

Christina Kim

AP Images

Christina Kim was almost twelve years old when her father, Man, took her into the backyard with her older brother and sister and introduced them to the game of golf.

"He said here's the stick, here's how to hold it, and here's how to swing it. Now swing it and don't stop," she remembers.

Man Kyu Kim, an immigrant from South Korea who settled in San Jose, California, had picked up the game himself about three years earlier, and fallen in love with it. Christina isn't exactly sure if her father just wanted his kids to get involved with a recreational activity that they would enjoy and that he could teach them, or if he had a master plan.

"I think his plan may have been to have my brother and sister and I play golf, get a scholarship to Stanford, and then turn pro. It could have been a circus act of Kims on tour," says Christina. Her sister shot par golf a year and a half after starting, but it was Christina who ended up outlasting both of her siblings and eventually becoming a winner on the LPGA Tour.

It was a very gradual and careful introduction into the game for the Kim kids. For a whole month, they swung about five hundred times a day in the backyard, hitting a plastic ball on a hook.

"It was only then that we found out there's a point to this whole thing. He told us there's a white ball and you try to hit it as far as you can and then hit it into a hole in as few strokes as possible," she remembers.

Focusing on the swing first, she says, gave her a better sense of rhythm. But even after the backyard swinging, Man's plan still didn't call for the kids to go to the golf course. The next step was the driving range. Christina remembers people being pretty impressed how well and how far they hit the ball, attention which fueled their enthusiasm. Still, it was two months of hitting at the range, along with lessons in the short game, before Christina, her brother Maeoll, and sister Gloria went out on the course for the first time.

Not that Christina questioned the arrangement. She never badgered her father to go out on the course.

"I was still very young and didn't know much about the game," she says. "I basically just did what my daddy told me to. In a South Korean family, you don't question what your daddy says, you just do it."

Man and his wife Dianna had come to the United States from South Korea in 1981, three years before Christina was born. Both had been schoolteachers in their native land, but Man ended up working for an electronics company in the Silicon Valley. Although he came late to golf, Man picked it up quickly. He broke 80 on his hundredth day of playing golf, and by the time he introduced his kids to the game, he was a plus-handicap very capable of shooting in the 60s.

Once Christina got to the course, the thing that most impressed her about golf was that she was surrounded by adults. "That was different than anything I had experienced. It was weird, but cool. Seeing people hit the ball that far and wanting to be like that was a neat experience."

Soon the summer arrived, and that meant total immersion. The kids would wake up early in the morning and head to a course about forty-five minutes from their home that had a junior program. They would spend the whole day there, playing as many as fifty-four holes and also spending time on the range, until their father picked them up at 6:00 PM.

"I started foaming at the mouth for playing golf," Christina says.

Kim's father was her only instructor. On weekday evenings, he would often work with her on the range. As she improved — which was rapidly — he made sure to play with her often on the weekends. Sometimes, though, he would play with his golfing buddies, at which point Christina's mom, also a pretty good player, would take Man's place in the family foursome with the three kids.

Christina considers herself a "range rat" who loves to hit balls. But she also describes herself as a feel player who is not into a technical breakdown of the swing.

"He knew that, so he made the golf game fairly simple for me," she says. "We used numbers to symbolize which part of the swing to think about. A draw would be 'one-two' and a fade 'two-three.'

Because I was so young, he didn't use a lot of technical terms. Only rarely did he video my swing on the range. He knew I would probably take the camera and start filming butterflies. I didn't get the technical aspect and I still don't."

Man Kim's understanding of the swing was based on Ben Hogan's book *The Five Fundamentals of Golf*. "That was his Bible. The book was in tatters when he was done with it," says Christina.

Man enjoyed teaching golf so much that he also introduced some other neighborhood kids to the game. He even took some initial steps toward becoming a certified instructor, but didn't follow through when he realized that getting PGA certification would also require spending a lot of time working in a pro shop.

While Man didn't use his video camera as an instruction tool on the range, he did take it onto the course when Christina played in junior tournaments. In fact, he became pretty well-known as the dad who taped every shot his daughter hit.

"Dad used to run through the trees like a yeti with a tripod. He would be out there with a backpack with extra batteries and extra tapes to make sure he got every shot," she says.

The purpose of the tapes was partly to capture memories and partly to allow her to look at how she was playing and see what she needed to work on.

"After every tournament, I would be forced to watch myself on television," Kim says. "That's probably one reason I refuse to watch myself on television now. I haven't even watched recordings of my victories."

Christina started playing in local tournaments almost right away. By the time she was fifteen, she was able to break par and ready for a higher level of competition. She didn't play in many national events because of the expense involved, but at fifteen she qualified for the US Girls' Junior. It was played all the way across the country in Maryland.

"It was a terrifying experience," she says. "It was my first time dealing with humidity, and I felt like my lungs were collapsing. Dad took time off from work to come, and he was taking it very seriously.

"I shot 86–86 in the two rounds, which were my highest scores in a year. I can look back on it and laugh, but it was such a horrifying experience that at the time I never wanted to leave California again."

But that tournament was an aberration. Kim's game was strong enough that she returned to the national arena and got some positive results when she was sixteen. At seventeen, she was medalist in the stroke play portion of the US Girls' Junior with a 133 total for two rounds. That included shooting a 62 that was the lowest eighteen-hole score ever shot in any USGA championship—and twenty-four strokes better than what she had managed two years earlier.

She had already gotten her first taste of the LPGA Tour when she tried to qualify for a tournament near her Northern California home when she was sixteen. She didn't make it, but she did get to play a practice round with LPGA pro Mi Hyun Kim and had her father caddie for her for the first time.

"I shot a 78, but it was an incredible experience," she says.

The next year, in addition to her medalist honors at the US Girls' Junior, she qualified for the US Women's Open and made the cut. That got her thinking, not only about playing on the LPGA Tour, but about getting there as quickly as possible. She started thinking seriously about skipping her senior year of high school to play the Futures Tour, a developmental tour for women players.

"My parents were schoolteachers, so education was a big thing," she says. "I was trying to juggle academics with playing golf. I grew up with encyclopedias in my bedroom. At school, I already knew a lot of what my teachers were saying. I would sit in class thinking, 'I could be working on my flop shot.'"

Christina talked it over with her parents, emphasizing that she could pass a high school equivalency exam and eventually go to college if she needed to (she ultimately did the former but hasn't needed to do the latter). She pointed out that women peak athletically earlier than men, so she wanted to make the most of being eighteen, nineteen, and twenty.

"I asked my parents what their thoughts were about it. I wasn't going to go into it blindly," Christina says. "They were apprehensive, but they supported my decision. In fact, my dad might even say that it was his decision."

She played the latter part of the 2001 season on the Futures Tour as a seventeen-year-old amateur, and then turned pro the next year. At the time, only the top 3 players on the Futures Tour money list earned LPGA Tour cards for the next season (now it is the top 10). Kim ended the year second to Lorena Ochoa.

"I told my father that Q-School was not an option. That's a horrifying experience and I never wanted to go through that," she says. "I knew how I played as an amateur, and I just said I'm going to win on the Futures Tour. I wasn't going to leave school for nothing. I had my path set in stone, and I wasn't going to let anything get in my way."

Kim headed out onto the LPGA Tour just before her nineteenth birthday, and quickly proved that she was ready for the big time. As a rookie, she ranked forty-ninth on the money list with $215,632, and in 2004, her second season, won a tournament and collected $636,490, good for fifteenth on the list.

Her father was at her side, serving as her caddie and helping with travel arrangements, just as he had done on the Futures Tour, having left his job behind and hitched his fortunes to those of his daughter.

"He's the best caddie I ever had," Christina says. "He knows my game and me better than I know myself. We had some incredible experiences. He caddied in the Solheim Cup [United States versus Europe], which was thrilling, and he caddied in both of my victories. Not a lot of people get those kinds of experiences."

Kim's first win came at the Longs Drugs Challenge in 2004, just a couple of hours from her home, the same event she had tried to qualify for four years earlier as an amateur.

"We had been on victory's door just about every week going into that tournament. I was getting frustrated and Dad was frustrated for me because he knew I was so close to winning and hadn't broken through," Christina remembers. "Coming down the stretch, he was able to keep me focused on doing what I do. He was doing whatever he could. We were reading putts as well as we've ever read them. There was an intangible thing in the air that is hard to describe."

Kim closed with a 65 in the final round to beat Karrie Webb, one of the best players in the game, by one shot. "I dropped to my knees and was crying. My dad dropped to his knees with me and cried. It was an incredible moment. I'm sure it was very fulfilling for him. To have it happen so close to our hometown, there were so many things going on at once. It was sheer brilliance."

Kim is a highly emotional and demonstrative player even when she isn't winning a tournament. That may have been awkward for her father at times.

"I'm a tumultuous person," she says. "I have a lot of emotions, both positive and negative, and I show them, which is funny for him. He's emotional, but he hates letting his emotions get the best of him. "

When Christina first started on the tour, she relied on her father to pick her clubs, because he knew her game so well. But eventually she started to show some independence in decision-making on the course.

"I would start making cheeky comments or pick a different club than he was suggesting," she says. "I'm sure that seeing a child grow up is tough as a parent sometimes. Finally, Dad said you are going to have to make your own decisions. It was tough for him, but he started letting go a little bit."

It was an interesting dynamic in the Kim household, which was permeated with the Korean culture of the parents but also influenced by American culture.

Christina admits that she was getting more Americanized all the time, but it wasn't until she turned twenty-one that she was able to establish her independence.

"I didn't really learn what it was to say no to my parents until I was twenty-one," she says. "I always appreciated that parents give up their lives to some extent because they want their children to have a better life. Whenever I had an issue, I would keep that thought in mind. But after twenty-one, I stopped doing that."

Halfway through her fourth year on tour, when she was twenty-two, Kim decided it would be better if her father didn't caddie for her anymore. "To be a better player, I had to learn to make my own decisions. The same thing in life too."

Man remains her only swing teacher. And it wasn't until 2010 that she went to anybody else for putting advice. That's when she saw Ron Stockton after being at wit's end about her putting. After meeting with Stockton, she nearly won the next week, losing in a play-off. Her dad didn't have a problem with Christina going to someone else; in fact, after seeing such rapid improvement in her putting, he said, "See him again."

After he stopped caddying, Christina's father continued to come to most of the tournaments, but now he has cut it back to about six events a year. Christina moved to Florida to facilitate travel to the LPGA Tour, which is mostly played east of the Rockies, and her parents followed her. They are mostly retired now, though Man is involved with a business in Korea.

Christina finished her eighth season on the tour in 2010, remaining in the top 40 on the money list in every season after her rookie year. When she comes home from the tour, she still plays regularly with her dad, and she still turns to him to iron out kinks in her swing.

"I wish I knew as much about myself as he does," says Christina. "Honestly, he's still my best friend."

Brittany Lincicome

Tom Lincicome made the ultimate sacrifice for a scratch golfer in order to give his daughter, Brittany, the best opportunity — he gave up the game.

"It was too expensive for both of us to play," says Brittany, now twenty-five years old and a three-time winner on the LPGA Tour. "He had to quit basically to support me and to travel."

The Lincicomes were a middle-class family in South Florida who ran a day care center. The only way they could afford for Brittany to travel the junior golf circuit up and down the East Coast (going west was out of the question) was to pour all of their resources in that direction.

Brittany was around fifteen or sixteen years old when her dad stopped playing. The goal at that time was not so much the LPGA Tour, but a college scholarship. The Lincicomes knew that with the dearth of teenage girls playing golf, scholarships for women's golf teams sometimes went begging. So, by sacrificing now, they figured, Brittany would get a college education they might not otherwise have been able to afford.

Brittany's involvement in the game began about five years earlier simply as a bit of family fun. When she was ten years old, she began joining her dad and her two older brothers for after-dinner outings at a lighted par-three course next to their home. Within a few months, she made her first hole in one, which one brother greeted with a great deal of enthusiasm and the other — who had yet to make one — less so.

"We're a competitive family," says Brittany. "Even today, if I go fishing with my brothers, I want to catch more fish or bigger fish."

Brittany quickly showed enough aptitude and desire for the game that in addition to the par-three outings, she spent time at the driving range and at the big course, all of which were located at the same public facility practically at their doorstep. Until she started playing in tournaments a couple of years later, she played nearly all her golf with her father and brothers. It didn't take very long for the athletic Lincicome to start hitting the ball far enough to play from the same tee markers as her brothers — and not much longer before she started beating them.

"That's probably why I hit it so far, from playing with all boys growing up," says Lincicome, one of the longest hitters on the LPGA Tour, averaging 270 yards off the tee to rank second in 2010.

It took a while longer to beat her dad, who, after all, was a scratch player. His advantage wasn't necessarily length, even though they were playing from the men's tees. Not a particularly long hitter, Tom was very accurate with a great short game — much better than Brittany's in her formative years.

"At first, it was just let's go out and play. When I got a little older, we started playing for silly things like taking out the trash or doing the dishes," Brittany remembers. "It was all for fun."

Still, Brittany couldn't help notice that her scores were getting closer and closer to her dad's, and finally one day when she was about fifteen, she was able to beat him. "Then I started beating him consistently and it was more fun," she says. It wasn't long after that when her father stopped playing. (He has now switched mostly to tennis, playing golf once or twice a year.)

Tom was naturally her first teacher when she started out, schooling her on the basics. As she improved, she began to see a swing coach, but Tom always observed the lessons so he could know what Brittany was working on and could spot any flaws.

"It's easier for him to spot things from the outside," says Brittany. "I can't always tell what I'm doing wrong."

When Brittany started playing in junior tournaments at age twelve, Tom was very involved. With Mom, Angie, staying home to run the family business, Dad shepherded Brittany to all of her junior events.

"Golf was more a Dad-and-I kind of thing. He understood golf and knew my swing," Brittany says. Mom's role was home-schooling Brittany, which she did from sixth grade through high school.

Brittany made her way up in the world of junior golf in stages. "I started slow. Dad said if we couldn't beat all the local girls, we wouldn't go to the next level," she says.

At around age sixteen, she made it to the American Junior Golf Association level, competing against some of the top juniors in the nation. It was like a different world, especially considering the backgrounds of some of the elite players.

"A lot of the girls went to one of the academies [special high schools where they concentrated on golf] or they had [noted instructor] David Leadbetter as a teacher," Brittany says. "They had nice clubs, nice clothes, Oakley sunglasses. It was definitely intimidating."

Lincicome had some strong finishes, but endured some hard times too. One time she missed a cut at a tournament in New Jersey—which was about as far from home as she ever played—and Tom drove her right back to Florida, twenty-two hours straight without stopping to spend the night.

On those occasions when she played badly, Tom always wanted to discuss what went wrong and give her advice on how to do better, but Brittany didn't necessarily want to talk.

"There were happy times and there were a lot of tears, depending how I played," she says. "I can joke with him now. Even now, at twenty-five, if I play badly or do something wrong, I hear about it. I say, 'Do you really think I hit it out of bounds on purpose?' It was harder when I was younger.

"I took it all in and listened to what he said. Sometimes there were frustrations. He had good advice sometimes, but you don't want to hear it when you're young."

Besides junior tournaments, Brittany played high school golf on the boys' team. Although homeschooled, she was eligible to play for the school in her district. This was another area where her parents sacrificed. The high school where she started out didn't have a good golf team, so after Brittany's freshman year, the Lincicomes sold the house they had lived in for fifteen years and moved to where Brittany could play for a stronger program.

The new team worked out well, but playing boys' high school golf wasn't always easy. "You can imagine being a girl, you weren't very welcomed," Brittany says. But, in a way, that made it more rewarding when she showed that she was just as good as they were, if not better. "It's fun when they think you can only hit it 200 yards and you step up to the first tee and hit it 280."

Her parents told her to ignore any resentment she might have felt from the boys. "They always said, 'Just beat them. They're jealous.'"

In the end, high school golf was a good experience. "Playing with boys helped me get to where I am," she says.

Next came a decision that was not easy. All along, the family had been shooting for a college scholarship. But Brittany had become so good, and could hit the ball such a long way, that they began to wonder if she should just turn pro right away.

"Dad had been keeping up with how some girls did, who went to college a couple of years earlier, and they had not been able to handle it. Some of them even ended up quitting golf," says Lincicome, who received some fifty scholarship offers.

Lincicome also felt uncomfortable about entering a college environment after having been homeschooled, and that was a factor in her decision to go pro.

"I made it to the tour right away, so it was a good decision," she says. "Still, when girls ask me about it, I always tell them they should go to college for at least two years. These kids think it's easy, but it's not. I got very lucky."

Even Qualifying School was an adjustment after junior golf. In junior and amateur events, Lincicome had carried her own bag nearly all the time. Now she enlisted her father as a caddie, and that took some getting used to.

"It was different. You're so used to doing your own thing, being in your own world," she says. "It's such an individual sport. But it was good to get a second opinion on how a putt would break."

It was also a different dynamic in the father-daughter relationship, with the girl now essentially being the boss, at least on the course.

"If he was saying too much, I would definitely tell him," Brittany says. "He's Dad and he always thinks he has the right answers, and he usually does. I always listen to what the caddie has to say. But I usually do what I wanted to do."

Lincicome made it through Q-School, thanks to a final-round 68, after being very much on the borderline throughout. The public course player without much of a national profile had made it to the biggest stage of all—at the age of nineteen.

"We had no expectations. We didn't know anybody who had done it before," says Brittany of her Q-School experience.

The celebration was muted because of the draining nature of the event. "It was more a sigh of relief," she says. "That's a grueling

Courtesy of Brittany Lincicome

five days of very stressful golf. We were both exhausted and just glad it was over."

Starting out on the LPGA Tour was a daunting experience. "I went from junior golf, where I knew everybody, to only knowing Paula Creamer," says Brittany.

Then there was the matter of having to travel from city to city every week, packing, arranging for hotel rooms and transportation, and the various small and large hassles that arise from life on the road. Fortunately, her father came along and handled all of the travel arrangements.

It was a different world for Tom too, especially in his role as caddie. At the orientation sessions after Q-School, Brittany learned that players would be fined if their caddie didn't rake a bunker properly. "We spent thirty minutes making sure he got it right," she says.

While it was beneficial financially, the Lincicomes found that having Dad on the bag was not an ideal situation.

In her junior days, Brittany sometimes had to take more criticism than she wanted to; now she was dishing it out. "It's hard. I don't know how girls have their husbands caddie for them," she says. "You're going to yell at your caddie whoever it is. But then after that, he's your dad, you love him, and you're eating dinner with him that night. It was tough drawing that line between caddie and father."

In her second year on tour, 2006, Brittany scored a victory in a big tournament, the HSBC Women's World Match Play Championship. The first place check was a substantial $500,000, enabling Brittany to summarily fire her dad as her caddie.

Not that she lost Tom as a traveling companion. Even to this day, he comes to about 90 percent of the tournaments (Brittany's mom makes it to about 50 percent). "He would die if I told him he couldn't come out anymore," Brittany says.

Tom continued to be very involved in his daughter's game. When Brittany had a swing coach, he would still attend every lesson, even after she was playing the tour, in order to be able to help her get back on track if she had problems with her swing. For the last couple of years, she has gone without a teacher, considering herself a "feel" player who doesn't like to get technical. While she is largely self-reliant, Tom's observations and suggestions for her swing carry some weight.

One thing he has a hard time doing is getting Brittany to practice. "Even to this day, I despise practicing," she says. Tom knows not to press too hard. "He understands that if I practice for an hour a day as opposed to ten, it's all right as long as I do it the right way."

But he also knows how to apply the needle. He tells her that if she dislikes practicing so much, then put in ten years and make a lot of money. *Then* she can retire.

Lincicome has collected more than $3 million in her first six years on tour. The highlight of her career so far came when she captured a major title at the Kraft Nabisco Championship in 2009, winning by one stroke with an eagle on the par-five finishing hole after hitting a spectacular second shot to within four feet of the cup.

The winner of the Kraft Nabisco traditionally jumps into the pond in front of the eighteenth green, sometimes accompanied by her caddie, friends, or family. Brittany made the leap with her dad and her caddie, Tara Bateman.

"Dad and my caddie had talked about it during the week," she says. "I heard some of that conversation, but I really didn't want to think about it. I didn't want to get ahead of myself."

While the leap was a celebratory moment, a quieter exchange a day later in their rented house was just as meaningful.

"We woke up the next morning, and he said, 'Can you believe what you just did?'

"I said, 'Pinch me, I've been dreaming.'"

It's a dream the Lincicomes could hardly have imagined fifteen years earlier during an evening par-three round under the lights in South Florida.

Kristy McPherson

Kristy McPherson grew up just outside of Myrtle Beach, South Carolina, a golf hotbed with courses galore. But instead of playing any of those local courses on a regular basis, she played most of her golf at a small club about a fifty-minute drive from her home.

While the Myrtle Beach courses are mostly geared toward vacationing golfers, unassuming Pine Country Club was a better fit for the McPherson family pocketbook. Membership cost only a couple hundred dollars a year, and even better, they let Kristy and her brother Kevin play for free.

The course wasn't a very challenging one, not the kind of place you would expect to produce a tour pro. But playing there did have an unexpected benefit. Those fifty-minute drives to and from the course were a perfect time for golf discussions that were just as beneficial as lessons might have been.

Kristy didn't like lessons anyway. "I had a couple of lessons when I was younger. Honestly, I'm a little too hardheaded and stubborn," she admits. "I wanted to do it my way. After a couple of lessons and it wasn't working, I said enough."

So, her father, David, became her only teacher, not just on the course but in the car.

Kristy wasn't a range rat by any means, so some of those discussions about the golf swing took the place of beating balls on the practice tee. "He would explain how to hit a low punch, a high fade, and different kinds of shots," she recalls.

A lot of the talk was about course management, and much of it involved reviewing and analyzing how she and her brother had played that day. Since they usually played fifty-four holes in a day, it's a good thing they had a long car ride.

"We would go through all fifty-four holes. You know how parents are, he would want to hear about the bogeys and why we made them. We were always talking about how to get better. I learned a lot on the weekends for sure," she says.

This was the second phase of Kristy's golfing life, spanning from age twelve through high school. She had been introduced to the game earlier, at around seven or eight. There was an active junior program in Myrtle Beach, and during the summers, Kristy and her siblings (two brothers and a sister) would attend junior clinics and play in junior tournaments.

"I played junior golf just because it was what you were sup- posed to do in the summer," says McPherson, who was very active in team sports the rest of the year. "I played a lot of basketball and softball. I loved the sports where you could yell and scream. Golf was a little too quiet for me."

But when she was eleven, McPherson began to feel a debilitat- ing pain and was diagnosed with a form of juvenile rheumatoid arthritis. She spent eleven and a half months mostly in bed, barely able to move, and was homeschooled in the sixth grade.

One of her first ventures back into the outside world after she began to get a little better was when her father took her to the golf course and had her ride in the cart with him. Kristy said to her father when they came to the tee at one of the par-three holes, "Daddy, make a hole in one." Believe it or not, he proceeded to fulfill her request.

"I thought, 'My God, this game is easy,'" Kristy says.

McPherson slowly recovered, but anything involving running and jumping was now out. That left golf. It took a while before she could even do that. First, she needed to learn how to walk again. Then she could chip and putt, then hit a few balls, then hit more balls, and finally she could play.

That's when the McPhersons joined Pine Country Club and started to play together there. But it was her freshman year in high school when Kristy really got serious about the game. There was no girls' team, so she tried out for the boys' team and made it.

"I hated losing to the boys because then I would have to hear about a girl being on the team. But they couldn't say anything if I beat them from the same tees. I loved beating the boys and I just wanted to get better and better," Kristy says.

"When I was a freshman, I was kind of cussing that there wasn't a girls' team, but playing with the guys is the best thing that happened to me. Playing with boys and playing from the back tees was the reason I'm able to play on the LPGA Tour today. It just gets easier from there."

When she wasn't playing with boys in high school, she was playing with men — again from the back tees — on weekends and in the summer. Kristy, her brother Kevin, and her dad were in a group of about forty regulars who got together for friendly competitions at Pine.

The main competition involved grouping into four-player teams with A, B, C, and D players, based on ability. The McPhersons were all A players, so they were never on the same team. But teammates didn't necessarily play together — the accounting of scores was done after everyone finished — so the family did play together for at least eighteen holes. This was a serious golfing group. The McPhersons weren't the only ones to play fifty-four holes; nearly everyone went around the course two or three times. Often, Kristy's father would switch out of the family group for one round to get involved in a money game with his friends.

"He was one of the best players there. If his score didn't start with a 6, he wasn't happy. Most of his rounds were 65, 66, or 67. He knew the course like the back of his hand," Kristy says.

David McPherson played college golf at Western Kentucky University and won numerous amateur tournaments in his native state of Kentucky. He moved to the Myrtle Beach area in 1979 with his wife Janice, a schoolteacher, a couple of years before Kristy was born, and started an electrical-contracting business.

According to Kristy, her dad is highly competitive and much prefers playing to practicing — traits she picked up. (She also says that they are both hardheaded and stubborn. They have similar gregarious personalities and the gift of gab too, so the apple didn't fall far from the tree.) They did spend some time on the range, but Kristy admits she didn't always listen.

"I was always stubborn. I would never do what he told me to do when he was there," she says. "Of course, I would work on it later. He was usually right, but you don't tell your dad he's right."

Many of those lessons involved getting rid of the big left-to-right hook that Kristy played with. Her father had overcome the same problem years earlier, so he was well qualified to help.

"When you know the course, you can hit as big a hook as you want," Kristy says. "But once you start playing in bigger tournaments on different courses, you can't do that. He would tell me, 'What you're doing is fine for now, but it isn't going to work down the road.'"

As Kristy and her brother Kevin developed in the game, they played in junior tournaments. Most of them were at the state level, but late in high school they played in some American Junior Golf Association events of national scope, although the family didn't have enough money for them to play in many of those.

Both parents went to all of the kids' junior tournaments, which was essentially their vacation. Most of the tourneys were on weekends, and since David owned his own business, he was able to take Fridays off if he needed to. David and Janice would split up, each watching Kristy and Kevin half the time.

"On the ride home, we were all golf," Kristy says. "We were always trying to look for a way to get better."

David was able to offer an insight to the competitive side of the game based on his experience.

"Competitive golf was a lot different than going out with the boys and playing on the weekend," Kristy says. "A lot of it is handling your emotions and nerves, trying to stay in your own game and not being influenced by the situation around you. Anytime you are trying to win an event, a lot of nerves come in. You've got to trust what you've been practicing and not let your emotions get in the way."

Starting out in some of the small, local tournaments without many competitors, Kristy might win with a score in the 80s. "He would tell me that was good, but you'll need to do better than that against stronger competition," she says.

By the time she moved up to compete against "name" players in AJGA events, Kristy's game was strong enough for her to be competitive, but she still found the events nerve-wracking. Her dad would boost her confidence. "He would say, 'You can compete with those girls just as much as you compete against the boys at Pine.'"

It turned out he was right. In fact, to her surprise, colleges began to take notice of Kristy. "Once I started getting recruited, I wanted to get better and better and get a full scholarship as a thank-you to my parents for their sacrifices," she says.

McPherson did get full scholarship offers, and ended up narrowing her choices to Furman, Auburn, and the University of South Carolina. Her role model, Beth Daniel, went to Furman, and that's where she started out wanting to go. But, after making her campus visits, she decided to go to the big state university a two-hour drive from home.

Her parents left the decision up to her. "They stayed out of the way, but they were definitely happy when I decided to go to South Carolina," she says. "It's close to home, and they were Gamecock fans."

They became even bigger fans, of course, when Kristy arrived on campus. Her parents attended nearly every one of Kristy's college tournaments. "They were good friends of the parents of a couple of the other girls on the team. They were the only parents tailgating before a golf event," says Kristy.

The first college tournament McPherson won was the Southeastern Conference Championship at the end of her sophomore year, with her parents and sister on hand to share the experience.

"It was really cool to see everybody get so excited at the end. My dad was saying, 'I knew she could do it.' That was kind of the breakthrough," says Kristy, who went on to win six more tournaments in her last two years.

David and Kristy continued to talk a lot at this time, but his role began to change as he became less of an adviser and more someone to simply share experiences with. "I was excited to call him and tell him about my rounds, especially the good ones," she says. "We talked about the good rounds more than the bad. He was very encouraging."

With her college record suggesting a future in pro golf, and her natural competitiveness leading her in that direction, McPherson made it through Qualifying School for the developmental Futures Tour as an amateur midway through her senior year of college.

"My parents said, 'If that's what you want to do, do it,'" Kristy recalls. "We probably had the talk about how tough it is, and you'll have to work hard. Only I don't think Daddy knew at the time how much it was going to cost him in the checkbook."

McPherson finished her college career that spring, and then headed into the world of professional golf with only her parents backing her financially.

"I had a couple of people who offered money to help get me going," she says, "but even though they were friends, we decided it was best not to be in the position of owing anyone. Dad said as long as we can do it on our own, we'll do it."

Entry fees are high on the Futures Tour and purses fairly low, so you have to be one of the top players to do better than break even. The way it worked was that you had to pay your fees for five tournaments in advance and then hope to play well enough to be able to afford the next five-event stretch. It wasn't easy for a middle-class family, but, between her parents' saving money and Kristy making every cut, they always managed to come up with the money.

"Sometimes it would run them pretty low," Kristy says. "It was extra motivation to play well enough to not put my parents in a bad spot."

Her mom and dad attended tournaments that were within driving distance and David caddied for Kristy a couple of times during her first half year on the Futures Tour. The last of those might even have saved his life.

When David caddied at an event in Pennsylvania, his hip was hurting as he walked the course. Meredith Duncan, one of Kristy's friends on the Futures Tour, said that her own father had just found out he had cancer and suggested that Kristy's dad should get checked out. David figured he had arthritis, but when he went to the doctor, he got the bad news. He had cancer that had probably been there for a couple of years. It had eaten into his hip so much that the hip was broken — he had caddied on a broken hip. He also had kidney cancer.

David got a hip replacement, had his kidney removed, and has been cancer-free since, though he has to walk with a cane. Doctors told him he wouldn't be able to play golf again.

"But he's just as stubborn as I am," says Kristy. "He was determined to play. He'll get out of the cart, walk with his cane to the ball, drop the cane down, and hit the ball. The first time I played with him, he was under par."

Kristy displayed her own stubbornness and determination in pursuing a spot on the LPGA Tour. Her stay on the Futures Tour lasted much longer than she wanted — three and a half years — due to a series of frustrating experiences at LPGA Q-School. The worst was her first attempt at qualifying. With three holes of her final round remaining, she looked like she was on her way to getting her card when play was suspended by darkness. The next morning she bogeyed all three holes and fell short by one stroke. The next two years, she missed getting her card by two strokes and one stroke.

"Dad and the whole family were very encouraging," Kristy says. "Time after time he had to say, 'Well, you know, your mom and I will come up with the money if you want to keep playing the Futures Tour.'

"There was one time I was calling around about trying to find a job, but I had some friends who said I was playing pretty well so I should stay with it. I was lucky to have parents and friends that were stubborn."

McPherson improved each year on the Futures Tour, and, in her final season there, she set her sights on finishing in the top 5, which would earn her an LPGA card without having to go through "that stupid Q-School," as she calls it. She was fourth on the money list at one point in the summer, but got a chance to appear on the Golf Channel's *Big Break* reality show. While missing two events, she fell to tenth on the list, but won a tournament to move back into the top 5.

Kristy ranked fourth heading into the final tournament in Albany, New York. With her whole family in attendance (except for brother Jared, who was in law school), she sweated out the end of the tournament. She wound up holding on to the fourth spot and getting a ticket to the LPGA. "It was a huge relief for everyone," she says.

McPherson headed to the LPGA Tour in 2007, still with her father's financial backing. The good news was that entry fees were a lot lower and purses a lot higher. The bad news was that expenses were much higher and making the cut much harder. Kristy missed the cut in four of her first six events, but finally made a few decent checks and finished the year with $79,724, enough to rank ninety-seventh on the money list and keep her card.

"After that, I relaxed, started playing better golf, and began to make money instead of breaking even," Kristy says.

McPherson made a big jump to $407,237 and forty-seventh on the money list in 2008, then really broke through in 2009 with a run-

ner-up finish at the Kraft Nabisco Championship, top 10 finishes
in two other majors, and earnings of $816,182 for sixteenth on the
money list.

Her dad was at the Kraft Nabisco, driving himself around the
Mission Hills Country Club in a little scooter because of his hip
problem. He was trying to decide whether he should drive the
scooter into the water to share the traditional celebratory jump into
the pond in front of the eighteenth green, but Kristy ended up losing by a stroke when Brittany Lincicome eagled the final hole. Still,
it was a proud moment for the McPherson family and a lucrative
one for Kristy.

Kristy was generous about sharing the wealth that came with
her success. That summer, she bought her father a fishing boat.
A few months later, she bought her parents a new house and her
mother a new car.

"They had been in the same house for twenty-eight years. I told
Mom and Daddy to find a house, and I would buy it. It was the least
I could do to help them after all they have done for me."

Her parents only come to a couple of tournaments a year now,
generally the Kraft Nabisco and a tournament in Mexico City that
allows caddies to drive carts—and thus allows David to caddie for
Kristy.

"He loves competitive golf and being part of it inside the ropes,"
she says. "He knows I'm an independent player, so I don't usually
ask for advice. When I do ask him something, he's excited to be part
of the game. But he kind of keeps his mouth shut."

It's not an easy task for a man with an outgoing personality.
"He knows more people than I know. It seems like he knows every
player, every caddie, every volunteer," says Kristy. "Everybody's
always asking me, 'How's your daddy?'"

Father and daughter were privileged to share a great thrill
when they got to play Augusta National, home of the Masters, in

the spring of 2010. It came about because Kristy's brother Kevin is now the women's golf coach at Augusta State, and Kristy donated money to the program. The school arranged for her to play Augusta National and said she could bring whomever she wanted. Who else was she going to take?

David had been slowing down, so he hadn't played in a while. He didn't have the energy to play every hole, but he made sure to play the iconic ones and recorded a birdie at the famous par-five thirteenth.

For a golfer, it doesn't get any better than that. For David McPherson, it was a sweet reward for raising a golf-coach son and a tour-pro daughter who appreciate where they came from.

Phil Mickelson

AP Images

W hen Phil Mickelson was born, his parents sent out a birth announcement that "Philip Alfred hurried to join the Mickelson threesome on the first tee at Mercy Hospital" and that after he was born, his first message was, "Let's play golf at my new home in San Diego."

Phil was truly born to play golf, but even his parents, Phil Sr. and Mary, had no idea that he would become one of the best players in the world. Nor did they know how close to the truth was their announcement that Philip came into the world ready to play golf.

When he was eighteen months old, Philip began to go out into the backyard to watch his father practice pitching and chipping. The large backyard was a feature that influenced the Mickelsons to buy this house when they sought out a bigger place as Philip was on the way to join sister Tina in the clan (a third child, Tim, was born seven years later). It was one of the best decisions they ever made.

For safety's sake, Philip watched his father from a face-on view. After about four months of this, Phil Sr. cut down the shaft of a wood to a length that could be wielded by a child still short of his second birthday. He showed his son how to stand up to the ball, right-handed.

"OK, now you can hit it," Phil Sr. said.

Philip immediately switched to the opposite side of the ball, changed his grip to a left-handed one, and took a swing, hitting the ball with the back of the club. From watching his father hit, he had developed a mirror image of the swing in his mind, and that's the way he wanted to do it.

"Well, that was a pretty good swing," Phil Sr. said, "but we've got a right-handed club, so come back over here." He tried to set Philip up to swing from the right side, but again the youngster switched to southpaw.

Observing that his boy was making an extraordinarily good swing for a toddler, Phil Sr. made a quick decision. Instead of messing with that swing, he would make the club left-handed. Fortunately, Phil Sr. had a workbench and the tools to turn what had been the back of the club into the face, and vice versa.

Philip was so attached to that club that he took it virtually everywhere he went. "It was like his teddy bear," Phil Sr. later said.

Philip couldn't even part with it at night. He went to sleep with the club by his side, and some golf balls too. When he woke up in the morning, the first thing he would do would be to go downstairs and into the backyard to hit his golf balls.

As a commercial airline pilot, Phil Sr. had stretches of three or four days off, affording him plenty of opportunity to get out in the backyard with his son and hit the ball around. One part of the yard was set up like a tee; they cut the grass short like a green in another part and dug a hole.

When Philip was three years old, his dad took him to a par-three course for the first time. Philip loved it, but he wanted more. He noticed that whenever his father planned to play golf the next day, he would put his golf bag next to the front door. So, Philip began to put his little set of four clubs next to his dad's and beg him to take him to the course and play.

Phil Sr. always said no, figuring there was no way the course would let a three-year-old on anyway.

Taking matters into his own hands, little Philip decided he was going to run away from home and go to the golf course on his own. He took his little golf bag, a little suitcase full of golf balls, his stuffed dog, and his favorite blanket. Philip got a neighbor boy of about the same age to accompany him on his journey.

This boy's Mom saw the two of them leaving and alerted a neighbor who came out to intercept them and ask where they were going.

"We ran away from home!" little Phil said. "And we're going to the golf course." After a pause, he added, "How do we get to the golf course?"

The neighbor told them to take a left at the corner and keep following that road. As it happened, that was a road that made a circle and came back to the Mickelson house, where both boys' Moms were waiting.

Not wanting his son to run away again, and seeing just how badly he ached to play golf, Phil Sr. decided to take him to the course after all. It took some convincing to let the manager of the Balboa Park municipal course let the kid on. But he finally relented and Philip took his place in a foursome that included his dad, his maternal grandfather, and a friend of his dad.

Young Phil was in seventh heaven, happily whacking his ball, running after it, and whacking it again, not slowing down the group at all. After two holes, he asked his father if he would carry his little bag, which he did.

Upon reaching the eighteenth tee, an uphill par five, Philip said he didn't want to play this hole. The adults assumed he was tired, but that wasn't it.

"Isn't this the last hole?" Philip asked.

"Yes."

"Well, if we play this hole, we'll be all done."

Phil Sr. convinced him that he had to play the hole, and his boy ran up the eighteenth fairway with the same kind of energy he had at the start.

The senior Mickelson later said that after that round, he felt his son was simply destined to play golf.

Phil Jr. received good athletic genes. His mother played basketball and his father was an Olympic prospect as a skier before enlisting and becoming a navy fighter pilot. After retiring from the navy to become a commercial pilot, Phil Sr. turned his recreational attention to golf, where he was a low-handicapper, and a very avid one at that.

Phil Jr. played other sports too, but golf was his passion. At the age of five, he won a putting contest at a week-long golf clinic, beating players as old as thirteen. He received a trophy, which he slept with that night.

Starting at the age of six, the Presidio Hills par-three course served as Philip's day camp during the summers. His parents befriended the owners, who agreed to watch out for the youngster when they left him at the course for the day. He would be dropped off in the morning with a bag lunch and $5—enough to cover the $4.50 all-day greens fee and two soft drinks.

Philip made his first birdie when he was seven. He also got his first set of clubs, which his father had promised in advance as a reward for finishing first or second in a junior tournament (he finished second). Left-handed junior clubs were hard to find, so Phil Sr. walked into a local golf shop and asked if they had any used ladies' left-handed clubs. He bought a set for $45 and cut down the shafts to Philip's size on his workbench.

The Mickelsons were a solidly middle-class family—public golfers, not country club members. Phil Jr. would soon start earning his own money to pay for future golf club purchases. Just as he got an early start in golf, this precocious kid got an early start in his working life. From age eight to twelve, he got a job at the Navajo Canyon public course picking up range balls and doing other odd jobs. The side benefits were free range balls and waived greens fees.

When Phil Sr. was home on a weekday during the school year, he would pick up his son for a late-afternoon round. Sometimes they played nine holes, sometimes as many as they could before it got dark—which could mean having to walk in from the thirteenth or fourteenth hole.

During one of those rounds, Philip got one of those lessons that kids often receive from their father about temper displays on a golf course. The eight-year-old uncharacteristically slammed his club into the ground after a bad shot. Then he did it again. And again.

After a warning, Philip banged his club yet again after missing a putt on the seventh green. Phil Sr. told him that since he obviously wasn't having fun, he needed to put his clubs in his bag and just walk along until he could start having fun. After one hole, Philip looked up and said, "Dad, I think I can have fun now."

Phil Sr. retired from the airline for health reasons in 1980, when Philip was ten. That gave them even more chances to play together. It was shortly after that when son beat father for the first time—by eight shots! At Navajo Canyon, Phil had one of his best rounds, a 73, while Phil Sr. had an off day and shot an 81.

Phil Jr. was dying to let his mom know as soon as they got home. But, he had been taught not to boast, so he waited for his dad to bring it up. And waited some more. Finally, he burst out, "Dad, aren't you going to tell Mom what happened?"

There were more father-son competitions in the backyard. Phil Sr. spent considerable time building a true practice green and bunker. The two would make up games, like taking twenty balls each and seeing who could hit the most shots within a flagstick length of the hole.

Phil Jr. also spent countless hours practicing on his own behind the house. Since there were trees, bushes, the bunker, various slopes, and enough space to hit a thirty-seven-yard shot, there were the opportunities to learn a variety of shots. Soon he began to notice how striking the ball in different ways imparted different kinds of spin and produced shots of varying heights and varying reactions when the ball hit the ground. "Sometimes my dad and I would try some crazy shots and then talk about why the ball did what it did. It was just fascinating to me," Mickelson wrote in his book *One Magical Sunday (But Winning Isn't Everything)*.

Of such practice was one of golf's most imaginative short games born.

Mickelson even began working on some trick shots in the backyard. As he was learning them, they didn't always come off as he intended. More than once, he struck the ball on a line instead of lofting it, or sent it squirting off in the wrong direction, resulting in a broken window in the house of his next-door neighbors, John and Barbara Peters. He always paid for the damage, and sometimes it took a while.

It's abundantly clear that Phil Jr. was not pushed into the game. If anything, his parents did their best to rein in his golf obsession and make sure he paid sufficient attention to schoolwork. Even in school, Philip managed to incorporate golf whenever he could. His sixth-grade science project investigated the difference between 80-, 90-, and 100-compression golf balls.

Sometimes Philip took things too far. The Mickelsons hosted a large family get-together one Thanksgiving and, itching to play golf on a day when the course wouldn't be crowded at all, fifteen-year-old Phil Jr. asked his mother if he could play. No, she told him, it was a family day and he needed to be home.

Phil didn't have a driver's license, but just as he had done twelve years earlier when he "ran away from home," he enlisted the same neighbor boy, Chris Peters, as a partner in crime. Chris had just turned sixteen and gotten his license, so Phil paid him $5 to give him a ride to the course.

He didn't arrange for a ride back because he pretty much knew what was going to happen. When the family sat down for dinner, Mary and Phil Sr. noticed that their oldest son was nowhere to be found—and neither were his golf clubs. Realizing what must have happened, they called the Stardust golf course, his regular haunt after he got a range-picking job there at age fourteen. Told that Philip was indeed on the course, and probably on the third hole by then, they walked out to the third green, met him, walked back to the car, and drove back to the family gathering.

Nothing was said until they pulled in the driveway and his mother talked about the importance of family. Phil Jr. conceded the point, but said that what he had in mind that day was a Ben Hogan saying, "Every day you don't practice is one day longer before you achieve greatness." It was a good-enough answer that he escaped punishment.

Philip's junior golf career was in full swing by then. It had really taken off when he made a choice between golf and baseball just before the summer he turned twelve. He consulted with his father before making the decision, and the discussion ranged as far ahead as the differences between playing the two sports professionally. In his book, Mickelson points to being strongly influenced by the fact that pro golfers are independent contractors. Undoubtedly, the fact that he could already shoot around par and had a bunker and green—not a mound and home plate—in his yard must have factored into the decision. Certainly, he made the right call.

Phil's retired father was able to travel with him to tournaments. Fortunately, he was the polar opposite of those notorious fathers who berate their kids after a bad round. Once, Philip shot an 88 on the second day of a two-day tournament in Tucson, after having been close to the lead following round 1. On the long drive back home, Phil Sr. started by saying, "What can we learn from today? Let's look at the bright side. There are a lot of things we can pick out and work on so that you'll be better next time."

"Together we talked about what to practice when we got home and how to play smarter in the next event," Phil Jr. recalled in his book.

As young Phil progressed and his travel schedule grew, his mother took an extra job to bring in more money. And his father's airline connection enabled Phil to travel for free, as long as he found a flight that wasn't fully booked. He started flying alone to tournaments when he was fifteen.

While their son definitely had an abundance of talent and had a pro career in his sights, his parents always sought to keep things in perspective. "We knew Phil had a special gift. But we always wondered what will happen when he gets older and meets up with other people with special gifts," Phil Sr. told *Golf Digest*'s Bob Verdi. "That's why we always stressed education and why we always held it over him that if he didn't do his chores, we would take his clubs away."

Phil Jr. was anything but a party boy in high school, as most of his time was taken up with playing, practicing, or working at the golf course. There was at least one occasion, though, when parental discipline was required.

Mickelson and his high school teammate Manny Zerman — whom he later beat in the 1990 US Amateur final — decided to spend an evening across the border in Tijuana, Mexico. Phil's car was side-swiped while he was there, and the ensuing delay caused him to miss his midnight curfew, an offense compounded by the fact that he didn't even call. Phil Sr. put up the chain on the front door so that his son couldn't get in.

Phil ended up sleeping on the front steps. "I wanted to at least give him a blanket," Mary Mickelson told *Golf Digest*, "but Phil [Sr.] said no, this is going to be a lesson for our son . . . We were probably stricter than we had to be because there weren't many times when Phil did wrong. But we can look back on it now and laugh."

Especially since Phil usually displayed a more responsible side. Phil told his parents while he was in high school that he definitely planned to go to college. He figured if he did go on to earn a lot of money as a pro, a degree in business would help him to manage it.

Phil ended up majoring in psychology instead, a field of study that may have served him just as well in future endeavors. He stayed all four years at Arizona State and got his degree, even though he had agents pounding on his — and his father's — door after he won on the PGA Tour at the Northern Telecom Open during his junior year.

"I had [International Management Group founder] Mark Mc-Cormack here on my couch," Phil Sr. told *Golf Digest*. "He talked about how Phil's marketability would never be greater and so on. I told McCormack I thought any corporation would be more impressed by a young man who finished what he started, college, than by a young man who won a golf tournament. I didn't want to speak for my son, but that's the way he felt too, and it seems to have worked out."

Mickelson waited to turn pro until graduating in June 1992, and it has indeed worked out, with thirty-eight PGA Tour wins including four majors. The third of those major titles came in 2005 at the PGA Championship, where he got up and down with a soft, high shot from just off the green on the seventy-second hole.

"This is no different from what I've done in my backyard since I was a kid," he said to himself as he surveyed the crucial shot.

No one was happier to see him pull off the shot than the man who fashioned that backyard practice area, Phil Mickelson Sr.

Jack Nicklaus

I t was a good thing for golf that Charlie Nicklaus decided to return to the game in 1948 after a long absence. Another fortunate
circumstance for golf, as it turned out, was that he required surgery on an injured ankle in the fall of 1949.

After spending three months in a cast, Charlie's doctor advised him to "give your foot as much movement as you can—the sort of movement you get when you walk on soft ground."

Playing golf sounded perfect for that. But when the spring of 1950 arrived and Charlie hit the course, he found out that he could only play a hole or two at a time without resting the ankle. Since golf carts had yet to come onto the scene—yet another link in this chain of events—he could not play with his friends at the club.

But he could bring his ten-year-old son Jack onto the course. The youngster had never really thought about golf before. A sports enthusiast, he was consumed by baseball in the spring and summer and football in the fall. But Jack was happy to tag along with his father at Scioto Country Club in Columbus, Ohio, toting a cut-down set of clubs and chipping and putting on the green while his dad was resting.

Charlie and Jack were very close. They had a comfortable relationship, one that allowed for some good-natured needling by Charlie that often produced the desired result. When Jack was in sixth grade, Charlie would constantly race him and rib his son about being beaten by a man with a bum ankle. With something to prove, Jack went out for the track team and by seventh grade was the fastest kid in his junior high school—and, perhaps more importantly, able to outrun his old man.

In golf, though, another man would have more of a hands-on influence. Scioto hired Jack Grout as its pro the same spring that ten-year-old Jack Nicklaus took up golf. That summer, Grout offered a two-hour clinic for juniors on Friday mornings. The young Nicklaus signed up for that and also took private lessons from Grout every two or three weeks. Grout would remain Nicklaus's teacher for the rest of his life, covering most of Jack's professional career.

The summer he was eleven, Jack got his first set of full-length clubs and began to work hard on his game. So hard that his father had to pay the price in range balls, as Jack went through at least ten buckets before and after each Friday's clinic. When the bill from the club would come, Jack related in his book *The Greatest Game of All*, "My father would say to me, half-frowning, half-pleased, 'From what I gather, Jack, most of the kids in the class hit out one or two buckets of balls. You, ten buckets, a dozen buckets. How does anyone hit out that many balls?'"

Such practice enabled Jack to break 80 for the first time the next summer, when he was twelve—shattering the barrier by six shots with a 74.

He broke 70 for the first time when he was thirteen in a round with his father at Scioto. Jack shot a two-under-par 34 on the front nine, and was surprised when his father said they had to go home for dinner. "Dad, we can't do that. I've got a chance to break 70," Jack said.

"I'll tell you what we'll do, Jack," his father said. "We'll eat and come back."

Jack protested that there wasn't enough time, but Charlie insisted, saying, "We'll do it my way." His father did cooperate by eating quickly and rushing back to the club, but daylight had just about run out when they reached the eighteenth hole. By that time, Jack needed an eagle on the par-five final hole to shoot a 69. He got it—by pounding a three-wood to the green in the near darkness and then holing a thirty-five-foot putt on a wet green where the sprinkler was already working.

That same summer, Jack won the thirteen-to-fifteen age division of the Ohio State Juniors as he embarked on a regular slate of tournament competition that included his first appearance at the US Junior Championship. Charlie was on hand for most of the tournaments and combined with Grout to give Jack the right blend of understanding, encouragement, and prodding.

The encouragement would often come in the form of Charlie passing along what Grout had told him. "Jack Grout tells me he never saw any young golfer more determined than you are to be a really first-class player," was a typical comment. On the other hand, when it was felt that Jack needed prodding, Charlie would point out what Bobby Jones had accomplished as a teenager.

Jones was a revered figure in both the Nicklaus household and at Scioto Country Club, where the great amateur won the 1926 US Open. On hand for that event was a thirteen-year-old Charlie Nicklaus. Young Charlie worked in a pharmacy and was given tickets by his boss, a man named Doc Mebs who also introduced him to playing golf. Charlie played high school golf, and posted scores in the 70s. But it wasn't his main sport. He was an all-around athlete who also played on the football, basketball, baseball, and tennis teams. He played freshman football at Ohio State and was in line for the varsity the next year when he was told that he needed an appendix operation in order to play football. But Charlie was focused on getting his degree in pharmacy and feared that recovering from the operation would hamper his studies, so he declined the surgery and ended his college football career (though he did play a little bit for the Portsmouth [Ohio] Spartans of the fledgling National Football League).

After graduation, Charlie worked as a salesman for Johnson & Johnson for seven years. In 1942, a drugstore near the Ohio State campus came up for sale, and Charlie got a couple of loans in order to be able to make the purchase. He had stopped playing golf in 1935, but decided to join Scioto and pick up the game again in 1948. Even with the country club membership, Jack later described his background as decidedly middle-class.

Jack was just like his father in that he had a chunky build but was very athletic. He ran track and played baseball up until his freshman year of high school, when he quit those sports in order to play on the golf team. But his favorite sport through most of high school was basketball, where he averaged more than seventeen points per game as a junior and senior.

He didn't completely forgo golf in the winter, though. Scioto erected a half Quonset hut that served as an indoor practice area, and at the same time Charlie Nicklaus built a similar "driving range" in his basement where Jack could hit balls into a mat.

Jack qualified for his first US Amateur in 1955 at fifteen. It was held at the Country Club of Virginia, and Bobby Jones was the speaker at the prechampionship dinner celebrating the twenty-fifth anniversary of his Grand Slam — winning the British Open and Amateur and US Open and Amateur.

Nicklaus was the youngest player in the field. That attracted the attention of Jones, who was a sensation himself when he was medalist at the US Amateur at the age of fourteen in 1916. During the practice rounds, he sought out Charlie and Jack for conversation. It was a thrill for both father and son, and one made even better because they found Jones to be down-to-earth and easy to talk to. But Jack felt some trepidation when Jones said he would watch his first-round match against Bob Gardner, one of the country's top amateurs.

Nicklaus was one up in the match when Jones pulled up to the eleventh tee in a golf cart. A nervous Jack promptly bogeyed the next two holes and made a double bogey on the hole after that, falling two down. Jones, realizing that his presence may have been making Jack try too hard, decided to leave at that point. Nicklaus made a comeback, but ended up losing, one down.

Later, Charlie Nicklaus and Jones would become good friends, spending much time together while Jack played in the Masters, which Jones hosted.

The most impressive golf accomplishment of Jack's high school years was winning the Ohio Open at age sixteen against a field that included professionals. During the spring of his senior year in high school, when he was seventeen, he had an epiphany when he realized that, while he loved basketball, what he really wanted was to be a golfer.

Nicklaus qualified for his first US Open that summer. He shot a pair of 80s to miss the cut at the Inverness Club in Toledo, but his dad helped him to keep his spirits up and Jack wasn't discouraged.

Three years later, Nicklaus would almost win the 1960 US Open as an amateur, stamping himself as a future star. That was during his time at Ohio State, his father's alma mater and the university where had known he was going since age six. He also won the 1959 and 1961 US Amateurs and the 1961 NCAA Championship.

Ever since Jack started playing golf, Jones was presented to him as the shining example to follow. So it is perhaps not surprising that he wanted to follow in his idol's footsteps and remain an amateur for life. By the time he finished at Ohio State, he was being called "the greatest amateur since Bobby Jones," a label that he enjoyed. Throughout the summer and fall of 1961, he told reporters that he had no intention of turning pro.

Jack had gotten a job selling insurance even before finishing college. He also got married while he was in college to fellow student Barbara Bash, and was insistent on providing support himself. "My father would have been only too happy to have helped out, but the day I got married was the last day I took a penny from him," Nicklaus wrote in *The Greatest Game of All*. "I knew he was there if I needed him, but it was time I tried to stand on my own feet."

Jack's income was less than $10,000 a year and his first child was born in September 1961. Given those circumstances, he knew that he had to at least consider turning pro. His sterling amateur record would no doubt earn him some endorsements, and he had every reason to think he would be near the top of the money list. What's more, even some respected career amateurs had told him that his game would develop to its full potential if he turned pro and played week in and week out.

"There were many ramifications to think about," Jack wrote. "I talked them over at length with Barbara and also with my father. He was, as always, just right with me. It was clear from our discussions that he was inclined toward my continuing as an amateur, but he presented his opinions without pressuring me and, at the close of each talk, reminded me that I had to be responsible for my own decisions."

After weighing all of the factors, Jack decided to turn pro. Instead of being the next Bobby Jones, he became the greatest player in the history of the game.

His father was a supportive presence for Jack at the majors until his death from pancreatic and liver cancer at the age of fifty-six in early 1970.

In *The Greatest Game of All*, published in 1969, Jack wrote of his father, "He is a very unobtrusive rooter. He makes it a practice to slide his name card out of his tournament badge, and he plods along outside the fairway ropes like everyone else."

Just in one instance did Charlie duck inside the ropes, and that was when gallery control broke down in the final round of the 1965 PGA Championship and Charlie wasn't able to see much. Near the end of the round, he slipped on a press badge he was carrying in case of an emergency and joined the reporters inside the ropes.

After teeing off on the sixteenth hole, Jack called out to his dad, "Hey, big boy, who are you covering for?"

"Evening News," Charlie responded.

Later that night, the two had a chuckle about it. "Evening News," Charlie said. "Can you imagine a duller answer?"

Nicklaus finished second in that championship, but handled himself with class in defeat. While he was one of the game's greatest winners, Nicklaus also was known as one of its most gracious losers, always available to the press and never sounding a sour note.

"As with so many things in my makeup, [that] derives from Charlie Nicklaus," Jack wrote in his autobiography *My Story* with Ken Bowden. "My father taught me the single hardest thing an athlete has to learn, which is how to lose gracefully. Dad convinced me very early in my involvement with sports that I had to accept the bad with the good; that, however much it hurts inside, you smile and keep a stiff upper lip; that you shake the hand of the man who's beaten you, and tell him congratulations, and mean it."

Charlie became ill in the fall of 1969 and died within a few months. Jack was devastated, but he was also spurred to rededicate himself to make a total commitment to being the best player he could be. He hadn't won a major championship in the past two seasons, and he realized that he was not working as hard as he should have been.

"As his decline continued, and knowing there was no hope, the emotion that surfaced more and more as I thought about our lives together was guilt," Nicklaus wrote in *My Story*. "Here was a father who had done so much for his son, who had seen what he believed to be a rare potential and who had struggled and sacrificed so selflessly to make that vision come true, and here now was the son, grown complacent, faltering, taking the easy way out . . .

"By the time Dad died, I had decided those days were over. I might never fulfill it, but now at least I had recovered the will to do everything in my power to live up to his dream."

Jack went on to win the 1970 British Open, getting himself back on track in a career that would finish with eighteen major titles—a career, and a life, that did fulfill his father's dream.

In his book *Jack Nicklaus: Memories and Mementoes from Golf's Golden Bear*, Nicklaus wrote, "As I grew up, I spent more time with [my father] than I did anyone else, simply because he wanted to spend time with me. He believed in me, supported the things I did, and he was always there for me, whether I needed a boost or a kick in the rear end. He rarely offered unsolicited advice about my golf game, but he was always there if I asked. I can't think of too many times when I didn't seek his counsel on important decisions, be it family, golf, business, or other matters away from the course. I can't think of any, really."

Perhaps Jack best summed it up with one sentence: "My dad was my best friend and I admired him more than anyone I've ever known."

Arnold Palmer

When Arnold Palmer was three years old, his father gave him a cut-down golf club and showed him the proper grip.

Kids tend to instinctively grab a golf club with a ten-finger baseball grip, but by putting a club in his hands so early, Deacon Palmer got around this problem — Arnold hadn't swung a baseball bat yet.

So he dutifully let his dad put his hands on the club with the Vardon grip, his right pinky overlapping the index and middle fingers of his left hand.

It's not the easiest grip for a youngster, but fortunately Arnold inherited his father's big, strong hands. Knowing no other way, young Arnie had a perfect grip from his very first swing.

Deacon Palmer (his given name was Milfred, but everyone called him by his nickname or its shortened form Deke) knew what he was talking about. He was the professional at Latrobe Country Club in Pennsylvania, about forty miles east of Pittsburgh. But don't get the idea that Arnold's golf swing was carefully constructed under his father's watchful eye. That wasn't the case at all.

On that first occasion, Deacon's only instruction aside from the grip was simply to hit the ball hard. Even as Arnold grew up, it didn't get much more involved than that. Deacon gave him a few fundamentals, but mostly left Arnold to figure out himself through trial and error the swing that worked best for him. And he continued to exhort his son to hit the ball hard.

This was during the 1930s (Arnold was born in 1929), when, although there were some notable swing theories, most golf instruction as practiced at courses and clubs around the country wasn't particularly technical. Deke hadn't entered the game from the teaching side. He was a working-class kid who got a job as a mail runner in a steel mill, but through a desire to work outside, he applied for and got a job on the construction crew building the new Latrobe Country Club.

When the course was completed in 1921, seventeen-year-old Deacon was asked to stay on and join the grounds crew. He had additional jobs running a poolroom and working in a steel mill for a while, but in 1926 he was named the superintendent at Latrobe. Somewhere along the way, he was taught the game by the club's first pro, a Scotsman. Deke worked himself down to a single-digit handicap and even began giving some lessons to members himself. With the Depression in full force in 1932, the club decided that it couldn't afford to have both a pro and a superintendent, so Deacon was asked to fill both roles. He remained in those roles for more than forty years, retiring as club pro in 1975, only a year before his death.

Deacon was very careful not to overstep his boundaries as a pro, not allowing himself or his family privileges that belonged to members. He never set foot in the locker room or dining room unless invited by a member, and ate his meals either in the kitchen or at home (the family moved into a house next to the sixth fairway in 1935, the year Arnold turned six). Arnold was never allowed in the club's swimming pool, and his access to the course was limited; he was only allowed to play when it was virtually deserted.

Still, young Arnold was a constant presence at the club. When he was seven years old, he broke 100 for the first time—and also made his first money playing golf. That summer he made a practice of hanging around the sixth tee when the groups of female members were coming through. There was a creek about hundred yards from the tee that some of the ladies had trouble carrying, and they began to pay him a nickel for hitting their tee shot over the water for them.

Arnold also used to chip shots out of the rough and trees into the fairways when there was nobody playing a hole. He couldn't practice chipping to the greens, because his superintendent father didn't allow that on the course (the restriction applied to members too) and Latrobe was a relatively humble nine-hole club that did not have a practice green. So, this was his way of practicing short shots. He later said that his time spent in the rough might have given him less fear of missing the fairway and contributed to his legendary ability to escape trouble as a go-for-broke pro.

The club pro's kid wasn't allowed to play golf with the members' kids, so when he did get onto the course, it was usually alone.

He would often play two balls, pretending that one of them was being played by one of the game's great pros. Arnold got to play with his father only once or twice a year.

When Deacon watched Arnold on the practice tee, his advice was usually quick and to the point. But he did give his son one enduring lesson, of sorts. "Almost from the moment he put that cutdown club in my hands, Pap [which is what Arnold always called his father] would tell me in no uncertain terms to let nobody fool with or change my golf swing," Palmer wrote in his autobiography *A Golfer's Life*, written with James Dodson.

Even as a professional, Arnold mostly followed that advice, and regretted the times that he strayed from it. "Anytime I ever got in trouble with my swing, lost the feel or touch in a shot, it was usually because I became enamored of some popular teacher's idea of the 'mechanics' of the golf swing and gave their advice a try, often really screwing myself up for a time."

While his swing advice was minimal, Deacon was thorough in instructing his son in the etiquette of the game and the proper way to behave on a golf course. He was a stickler for adhering to the rules; there was no rolling the ball on the fairway to get a better lie. As course superintendent, he was constantly preaching about the importance of replacing divots in the fairways and repairing ball marks on the greens. And he also imparted the necessity of respecting the game and your opponent: remaining still when your opponent was hitting a shot, congratulating your opponent on a good shot, and not outwardly displaying frustration after your own bad shot or defeat.

Deacon's strictures about the right way to do things extended beyond the golf course. He was adamant that, in the company of grown-ups, children didn't speak unless spoken to, he was big on table manners, and insisted that hats be taken off indoors or in the presence of women.

The discipline was more than just rules, though. "It wasn't the kind of discipline that just says what you can't do . . . It was the kind that said what you *had* to do—always do everything as hard and as well as you can," Arnold wrote in his first autobiography, *Go For Broke*.

Arnold did plenty of work at the club when he was growing up. After taking Arnold with him on the tractor when he was as young as three or four, Deke sent him out to work on the tractor on his own at age seven or eight. Within a few years, Arnold also started pushing heavy greens mowers, cleaning out ditches, planting trees, and other physical work.

When he was eleven, Arnold joined the club's caddie corps. He knew the course better than any caddie, but that didn't necessarily make him the best caddie. While his father had successfully gotten the point across to him that a caddie's role was not to offer advice unless asked, Arnold's expressive face often revealed his displeasure if a player chose what he felt was the wrong club.

One of the benefits of caddying was being able to play with fellow caddies on Mondays, when the course was otherwise closed. Arnold also was eligible for the caddie tournament, which he won five times. But his father never let him keep the trophy; he didn't think that would have been right for the pro's son.

Arnold's least successful job at Latrobe was working in the pro shop. When he didn't think there was anybody around, he would close the shop and go practice. After getting caught at it several times, including at least one occasion when a prominent member approached the shop and found it locked, he was summarily dismissed from that position. The Palmer boy's devotion to practice did pay dividends on the golf course, however.

By the time he was thirteen, Arnold was shooting near par at Latrobe despite having a relatively weak short game, the result of his lack of chipping and putting practice. This shortcoming was not entirely due to the club's lack of facilities. Deacon installed a putting green in the family's backyard to serve as a test for the grass used on the course, but Arnold was much more fond of practicing full shots and didn't use it all that much.

When Arnold first started playing, Latrobe was a par-34 course with seven par fours and two par threes. Before his teen years, some land was purchased to extend two of the par fours to par fives and make it a par-36. (Latrobe did not expand to eighteen holes until 1964.) The course was constantly being worked on by its superintendent and pro, Deacon Palmer, who over the years planted trees and made whatever other improvements he could on a limited budget.

Arnold was able to expand his playing horizons, thanks to his talent, which got him into junior tournaments around western Pennsylvania. His first tournament was at age twelve, and he really started with a busy summer tournament schedule at thirteen. His mother was the one who drove him to most of the tournaments, since Deacon wasn't able to get away from his duties at the club, but his father did make it to the ones played in town.

Deacon wasn't always impressed when Arnold returned from a tournament and told of his exploits. "He would typically nod and remind me with a sobering note of skepticism not to get too cocky and to keep practicing if I knew what was good for me," Arnold wrote in *A Golfer's Life.* "I must admit, I really burned inside to earn a simple compliment from my father . . . But that compliment never came, which probably explains why I tried all the harder to please him."

Strong in the upper body, Arnold had early aspirations of playing football. But as a freshman in high school he was still too small and he didn't make the team. That was fine with Deacon, who saw his son's golf potential and didn't want him to spread himself too thin. "If you want to be good at something, Arnie, you can't play a dozen things," he said.

The next year, the football coach wanted Arnold to come out for the team. But by then the teenager knew he wanted to concentrate solely on golf and he was no longer interested.

When he was fifteen, Arnold had a chance to play in an exhibition when the great Babe Didrikson came to town, with his father and a promising young player named Pat Harrison filling out the foursome. It was an experience that made Arnold realize how much he enjoyed performing in front of crowds.

Another experience at fifteen was less pleasant but also served as a valuable lesson. Arnold played in the West Penn Junior, with his dad and mom both on hand for the final match. Although he went on to win the tournament, at one point in the match he became so frustrated that he threw his club into a tree. When he got into the car for the ride home, Arnold was greeted with stony silence.

His father finally spoke during the ride. "If you ever throw a club like that again," he pronounced, "you'll never play in another tournament."

Arnold believed it—and he never threw another club.

Nine years later, Arnold enjoyed a considerably warmer post-tournament moment with his father. In the interim, Arnold had seen a lot: continued success in high school and junior tournaments; a promising career at Wake Forest that was cut short when he left school, devastated by the death of his best friend Buddy Worsham in a car accident; a three-year stint in the Coast Guard; and a return to the amateur golf scene while working as a paint salesman.

He made the field for the 1954 US Amateur at the Country Club of Detroit, and when he won the quarterfinals on Thursday, his parents got in a car that evening and headed for Michigan. Stopping for only a three-hour night's sleep at a motel, they arrived in time for Saturday's semifinal match, which Arnold won in extra holes. The next day, he beat one of the nation's top amateurs, forty-three-year-old investment banker Robert Sweeny, one up in the final match.

Celebrating on the green, Palmer called out, "Where's my father? Let's get Pap in here. He's the man who really won the US Amateur."

As the cameras clicked around them, Deacon put his hand on his son's shoulder and squeezed it. "You did pretty good, boy," he said.

As compliments go, it seems pretty modest on the surface. But coming from Deacon Palmer, it was high praise indeed.

"This meant the world to me, and I felt my own tears coming," Arnold wrote in *A Golfer's Life*. "I'd finally shown my father that I was the best amateur golfer in America."

Shortly after the US Amateur, Arnold met his future wife, Winnie, and they were engaged within days. The wedding was planned for the spring, but Arnold's dad had a lot to do with its happening sooner than that.

Arnold decided that turning pro was in the best interest of supporting his future wife. Accompanied by Deacon, he headed down to Miami to play in a tournament that November. On one of the practice days, Arnold found out that an old female friend, a model, was in town, and they went out for drinks. There was no romance involved, but when Arnold returned after midnight, he was confronted by Deacon, who asked if he loved Winnie.

Assured by Arnold that he did, Deacon responded, "Then you better go get her and get married and get on with your business and quit screwing around like a college boy. Do you understand that?"

Arnold understood. The next day he dropped his dad off at the airport to get back to Latrobe and drove sixteen hours to Winnie's hometown of Coopersburg in eastern Pennsylvania. Since Winnie's father wasn't ready to give his permission, the couple eloped and got married in Virginia.

Palmer won in his rookie season of 1955 and captured his first major championship in 1958, ushering in a period when he was the dominant — and most charismatic — player in the game. He retained his roots in Latrobe, building a house there (to this day, he still has a home in Latrobe, splitting time between Pennsylvania and Florida). When not playing the tour, he would hit balls for hours at the Latrobe Country Club range. As always, Arnold mostly worked things out for himself, with a few small tips from his dad.

While Deacon was proud of his son, he continued to keep him humble. In the 1967 book *The Evolution of a Legend*, author Mark H. McCormack quotes Arnold, "Every time I try to hit a cute shot of some kind, he'll really scoff. He doesn't think I am playing well unless I beat the ball to death . . . My overriding philosophy of the game, to hit it hard, comes from him. But I have never hit it hard enough to suit him."

In 1971, Arnold's success on the tour enabled him to buy Latrobe Country Club. Asked if he would retain Deacon as pro and superintendent, Arnold responded, "If he behaves himself."

Deacon stayed on the job but succumbed to a fatal heart attack in February 1976 while spending the winter at the other course his son owned, Orlando's Bay Hill. His ashes were spread — where else? — on a knoll above the eighteenth green at Latrobe Country Club.

Kevin Streelman

Courtesy of Kevin Streelman

Golf was very much a family affair for Kevin Streelman when he was growing up in the suburbs of Chicago. At least once a weekend during the golf season, sometimes twice, he and his parents would head out to the course.

It wasn't always the same course. The Streelmans didn't belong to a country club, but the Chicagoland area is known for its diverse array of fine public courses and they took full advantage.

"We would find a course that had decent twilight rates and go play," says Streelman. "We played a lot at Cantigny and Arrowhead in our hometown of Wheaton. But over the years we played most of the courses in Chicagoland. We would go to new ones to find out the ones we liked most."

Once a year, as a treat, they would play Cog Hill's Dubsdread course, the top public layout in the area and site of Chicago's stop on the PGA Tour. So it was a disappointment to Kevin, when he made it onto the tour in 2008, that the tournament had been moved to St. Louis that year. It was back at Cog Hill in 2009, but Kevin didn't qualify for the event, part of the PGA Tour's four-week FedExCup play-offs. Finally, in 2010, he qualified and got to play at Cog Hill as a PGA Tour player. Not only that, he nailed down a spot in the top 30 to qualify for the Tour Championship, which gets him into all four majors in 2011.

"There's nothing better than that, to have my parents there and all their friends. We had hundreds of tickets to give out. It was awesome, a really special week. My parents [Dennis and Mary Lou] told me how proud they are of me," Kevin recalls. "And one of my first thoughts on qualifying for the Masters was that Dad can caddie for me in the par-three contest on Wednesday. It's going to be a pretty teary couple of hours. It will be the ultimate."

Dennis Streelman first picked up the game when he was at officer training school in Germany. After serving in Vietnam as an army captain, he returned to the United States and took up the game with a passion, becoming as low as a three- or four-handicap.

Kevin arrived ten years after the second of his two other siblings, so by the time he reached golfing age, he was the only child in the house. He started playing at around nine or ten. At first, his parents would drop a ball for him at the 100-yard marker and let him play from there. He progressed through the 150- and 200-yard markers, and then the women's tees for a while.

Around seventh or eighth grade, Kevin began taking the game more seriously. While still playing basketball in the winter, he gave up soccer and baseball as his warm-weather sports to concentrate on golf and tennis.

"I liked that golf and tennis were individual sports, so you got all the glory—or all the shame," he says. "And the thing I loved about golf was that there are no two courses alike in the world. The playing field is always different." The latter view was no doubt influenced by playing so many courses as he was introduced to the game.

By the time Kevin entered his freshman year of high school, he was shooting in the 70s. Blessed with natural talent and with a desire to work hard to improve, the decision was made to start sending Kevin to a golf instructor.

"In order for me to take lessons, Dad stopped taking lessons himself," Kevin points out. "He sacrificed himself for me."

Not only that, but his father was determined to send Kevin to the best teacher in Chicago and did a lot of research to find out just who that was. The result was that Kevin went to Dr. Jim Suttie, a nationally known teacher who made his name working with Paul Azinger.

With Suttie's help, Streelman's scores improved from the high 70s as a freshman to the low 70s as a sophomore and junior, and entered the 60s as a senior.

"Even today, while I have another teacher, Dr. Suttie still helps me out when I see him once or twice a year out on tour. He will take a quick look and know what to look for," says Streelman.

As a sophomore in high school, Kevin began beating his father with both playing from the back tees. The first time it happened, says Kevin, his father "couldn't have been more proud. He got a kick out of it."

While the family rounds were much more about enjoyment than competition, they were spiced up during the time when they were shooting similar scores. "We had a lot of fun with it," Kevin says. "We wouldn't rub it in each other's faces, but we would jab at each other a little bit."

For her part, Mom enjoyed watching the friendly competition while playing her own game.

"Mom shoots between 100 and 110 virtually every time she plays," says Kevin. "Nobody loves golf more than she does. She'll never practice, but she'll go out and play all day if she can."

The family rounds continued through high school. While Kevin had a fairly busy schedule of high school practices and matches in the spring and junior tournaments in the summer, most of his casual rounds were played with his parents.

Kevin notes with some amusement that as his high school years progressed, his father sometimes started moving up to the regular tees in order to give himself a better chance to hit his drives past the ones his son hit from the back tees.

"He doesn't like to be outdriven," says Kevin. "He's sixty-seven now and he has no shame about playing from the senior tees, even though he still probably hits it 250 yards. Some of my friends who play with us give him a hard time because he's playing from the senior tees and hitting it past us."

Dennis tried to impart some lessons about course management during the family rounds, although Kevin admits that they sometimes fell on deaf ears.

"I was a pretty aggressive player. I always liked to go for par fives in two, no matter what. He would always tell me to back off and be smart," Kevin says. "As a high school kid, I thought I knew best. As I've gotten deeper into this as a profession, I have found out that he was right all along."

In addition to playing the game together, Kevin and his parents would gather around the television for the Masters and other major championships. "We used to love watching those," he says. "It was definitely my dream to play the Masters. I'm sure we did talk about me wanting to play there someday."

The first steps on that long road were high school and junior tournaments. Kevin played in a lot of Illinois Junior Golf Association events in the summer. He was often driven by his mom, but Dennis, who owned a medical consulting company, came when he was able to.

"They were very supportive. They couldn't have been there more for me," Kevin says. "They would drive to tournaments that were pretty far away. They would be there for high school tournaments where no other parents were there."

Streelman didn't play much on the national junior circuit, but he did finish second in an American Junior Golf Association event in Wisconsin. That got him into a bigger tournament, where he drew the attention of Duke golf coach Rod Myers.

His college choice came down to a decision between Duke, Northwestern, Vanderbilt, Miami of Ohio, and Wisconsin. Kevin's parents made all of the campus visits with him, and were involved in the final decision.

"Duke [in Durham, North Carolina] was the warmest place and also the best education. It really came down to affordability. When Duke offered a partial scholarship that was to the point where we could afford it, that's when we made the decision," says Kevin. "Deep down maybe they would have liked me to stay closer, but they knew that being able to play during the winter was a neat opportunity for me. After growing up in the harsh winters of Chicago, it was very desirable to be able to play the whole year."

Streelman's mom and dad were able to make it to a couple of his college tournaments each year. Kevin had a good college career, but was not an All-American, so he didn't come out of Duke with surefire pro credentials. But a talk with his father inspired Kevin to follow through with his pro tour aspirations.

"We had a big talk after graduation about what I wanted to do," says Kevin. "He sat me down and said, 'Kevin, you have to go after your dreams. You don't want to look back after thirty years and wish you had done it.'

"He was a very good baseball player who had been drafted to play in the minor leagues. But a couple of weeks after that, he was drafted to go to Vietnam. He wanted to be sure I gave it my all and worked my butt off to see what I could do in golf. I've never forgotten that talk."

Dennis also offered the financial support for Kevin to get his career off the ground. "He gave me ten thousand dollars to get started, which was all he could do," Kevin says. "It meant the world to me how much he believed in me and stepped up when no one else would."

That stake in 2001 helped enable him to play on a mini-tour in the Dakotas and go to PGA Tour Qualifying School, where he missed making it to the final stage by a shot. That winter, he returned home to live with his parents, work as a substitute teacher, practice at an indoor golf facility, and line up financial backing.

What followed were six more years on the minitours and several groups of sponsors — one of which abandoned him and left him stranded in California with almost no money.

"You hear about Tiger Woods or Phil Mickelson making it big right away, but for 98 percent of us there are a lot of tough roads that lead to the PGA Tour," says Streelman. "There were times when I would come home broke and try to find more people to believe in me, and my parents would take me in as long as I needed. They always had my back."

There was one occasion when Kevin was about ready to give up his dream of the PGA Tour. In 2003, the assistant coach job at Duke came open. "I was out of money on the minitours, and I said this will be a great job," says Kevin.

He sent in a résumé, got called in for an interview, and was one of two final candidates. He didn't get the job.

It happened that he got the bad news the week before the PGA Tour's Western Open was being played at Cog Hill. His father gave him $400 to enter Monday qualifying, which offered four spots in the field — and Kevin got one.

"That was the turning point," Kevin says. "The week before was the low point. And then all of a sudden I'm playing in a tournament on the PGA Tour. And I saw that those guys are really good but I can hang with them."

For years, Streelman couldn't even crash the Nationwide Tour, but he persevered, and in 2007, he made it through Q-School to land on the PGA Tour the next year. A month into the season, he found himself in the final pairing with Tiger Woods in the third round of the Buick Invitational at Torrey Pines. And that June, he led through the first round of the US Open, also at Torrey Pines.

Kevin rejoined the pack in the second and third rounds, but had a decent final round. During that round, he got the idea to have his father caddie for him on the eighteenth hole.

"I told my mom to have Dad be sure to be near the walkway close to the eighteenth tee box. When we got there, and I saw him, I told my caddie to give his bib and my bag to Dad," Kevin remembers. "He said, 'Are you sure I can?' and I assured him it was fine.

"Then he said, 'OK, I'll caddie for you, but you've got to be sure to make a birdie.' I flushed a drive and a three-wood, which ended up bouncing over the green [on the par-five hole]. Then I chunked my chip shot and left myself with a twenty-foot, downhill putt for birdie.

"I actually hit it too hard, but somehow it hit the back of the cup and went in. The place went crazy and Dad ran across the green and gave me a big hug. To share that with him, that was a cool Father's Day moment."

It wasn't the first time that Dennis caddied for Kevin. He's done it a few times for eighteen holes, most notably when Kevin shot a 62 at Aurora Country Club near Chicago in a local qualifying round for the US Open a few years ago (that round got Kevin into sectional qualifying but he didn't make the Open).

Kevin's parents have made it out to eight or nine tournaments a year since he's been on the tour. Two of the most meaningful were the Barclays in 2008 and 2010, both played at Ridgewood Country Club in New Jersey, near where Dennis and Mary Lou both grew up. Given the family connection that spurred Kevin in the game, perhaps it is no coincidence that in those weeks he produced two of his best showings on the PGA Tour, finishing fourth and third in the big-money event that kicks off the play-offs.

Looking back on his upbringing, Kevin says that his father was "a military guy, very organized. He wasn't too strict, but he was firm. He likes things done his way and the right way. But deep down, he's a teddy bear. He has more love in him than most people I've ever met and he would do anything for his children. I've never heard a bad word about him."

Tom Watson

At the age of six, Tom Watson learned the fundamentals of the game — and more — from his father, Ray.

On the range at Kansas City Country Club, Ray put a cut-down five-iron in his young son's hands. "Son," he said, "turn that hand over so you see two knuckles on the left hand. Point the

V that's formed between your thumb and forefinger toward your right shoulder."

With Tom taking the proper grip, Ray held his son's head as he stood over the ball and said, "Hit it."

"I kept my head pretty steady, and started getting the ball in the air," Tom recalls. "He did a great thing next. He said, 'I'm going to teach you how to hook the ball and slice the ball.'

"It gave me a feeling for how to control the ball. It was like teaching a kid to throw a curve ball when he just started to throw."

That cut-down five-iron had a hickory shaft, even though steel-shafted clubs had been in play since the 1920s and had become quite common a couple of decades before Tom got his start in the game as a six-year-old in 1956. But the pro still had on hand a number of hickory-shafted sets that members had traded in, so that's what youngsters often started with.

That first golf club might have been rudimentary, but young Tom had a lot of advantages, starting with the country club membership that Ray's successful insurance business enabled him to provide the family. What's more, Ray was a very accomplished amateur golfer himself. He advanced to the quarterfinals of the 1950 US Amateur, where he had Frank Stranahan, one of the top amateurs of the day, on the ropes before losing one down.

Ray was on the winning pro-am team at the 1941 Bing Crosby Pro-Am, which was then played near San Diego. He was preparing to follow in the footsteps of his father and grandfather and become a lawyer, but service in World War II got in the way.

"He later told me, 'Son, that was the greatest thing that ever happened,'" Tom recalled. "'First, I didn't get killed. Second, I didn't want to be a lawyer.'"

Ray was a club champion at Kansas City Country Club, where he once shot a 64.

He didn't compete much outside of Kansas City, entering only a couple of US Amateurs. But he played spirited matches with his regular Saturday foursome at the club, which had a great influence on Tom's development.

Tom started caddying for his dad in those regular games when he was nine. That was the same time he decided to get serious about golf after being cut from the midget baseball team he was trying out for.

"Kids don't get cut anymore. They don't want them to be disappointed," Watson says. "But back in those days, you had to deal with your disappointment. The way I dealt with it was focusing on golf."

A couple of years later, Tom had gotten good enough that "I guess my dad wanted to show me off," and he started joining the regular games as a player.

There was always a dollar Nassau on the line, and young Tom was always in on it, though his father or his dad's friend Bob Willits would cover for him if he was on the losing side.

"Every shot counted," Watson says. "That's one of the things that steeled my competitive fire."

Watson told *Sports Illustrated* in 1995 that those matches were at once collegial and competitive, and so "I learned how to needle and how to take the needle, how to laugh and have fun. But all the people who played golf with my dad were serious golfers—serious meaning they loved the game. Every time they hit a golf shot, they were there for one purpose only, and that was to hit it the best they could."

Watson considers himself fortunate that Kansas City had a good program of junior tournaments, so he got to play all over the city.

"One of Dad's great comments was that anybody can be great at one golf course, but if you learn to play at other courses, you can be a good golfer," Watson remembers.

At fifteen, Watson played in an exhibition with Arnold Palmer. "Dad asked him what the best thing would be for me to become a great golfer, and Arnie said, 'Compete as much as you can.'"

By that time, Watson had already won the Kansas City Men's Match Play Championship. At fourteen, he beat a man twice his age in a grueling thirty-six-hole final on a hot day.

"After I won, the understated pride of my father was palpable as he hugged me and simply said, 'Well done, son,'" Watson remembered in a blog item posted on his website (www.tomwatson. com) in 2010.

Watson started out trying to swing like his father, or to some extent like Sam Snead, because he was the player that Ray most admired. But at the age of eleven Tom started working with the club's new pro, Stan Thirsk, on a swing that was more upright and patterned after Jack Nicklaus. Thirsk would become his longtime teacher, but Ray still had his own observations, sometimes blunt ones.

Watson says his father "didn't suffer fools gladly," and he was the same way with mediocre golf shots.

"Even if the result was good, if the contact wasn't good, he would say, 'You didn't hit that. You hit that off the toe,'" Tom remembers.

Once, Tom got angry and threw a club, breaking the shaft. It wasn't in front of his father, but Ray found out about it.

"He said, 'That'll be ten bucks," Watson recalls. "That was a lot of money when a dollar a week was your allowance. He made it clear that behavior has consequences."

Ray also knew how to motivate his son, telling him he would give him a dollar when he broke 90 and another dollar when he broke 80. Watson doesn't remember when he broke 90, but he shattered the 80 barrier when he was thirteen, shooting a 76 at a short par-72 course.

There were occasions when Tom learned first-hand just what a competitor his father was, most notably in a couple of memorable matches at Walloon Lake Country Club in Northern Michigan, where the family would go for summer vacations.

When Tom was fourteen, he faced his dad in the finals of the Walloon Lake club championship. Tom was two up with three holes to play in the match-play event, but Ray made up the deficit with a birdie on the sixteenth hole and a par on the eighteenth, sending the match to extra holes.

Tom hit a good drive on the first hole, while Ray drove his badly, couldn't reach the green with his second shot on the par four, and ended up facing a twenty-five-foot putt for a par. Tom, meanwhile, hit his approach to fifteen feet and had a chance for a birdie.

"I was thinking, 'I've got him here,'" Tom remembers. "Then he made his long par putt and I missed my birdie putt."

On the next hole, Tom again hit the green in regulation and Ray missed. But Ray chipped the ball within tap-in distance for a gimme par, and Tom ran his first putt three feet past the hole. No fatherly generosity was forthcoming; Ray didn't give the putt to his son, and Tom missed it to lose the match.

"I think his message was that nobody's going to give you anything—you have to earn it," Watson says.

The next year, father and son met in the final again. A year older, wiser, and further advanced in his game, Tom was too much for his dad this time, winning three and two.

"We were competitors. In those matches, we wanted to beat each other in the worst way," Tom says. "I probably wanted to beat him more than he wanted to beat me, but still that wasn't reason for him to give me that putt."

Watson recalls playing as partners with his father once, at the Heart of America Four-Ball while Tom was in high school. It was in late summer, after Tom had started football practice (he was a quarterback on his high school team), and his muscles had some trouble adapting back to the golf swing.

"That's the only time I cold topped the ball off the first tee," Watson says. "But Dad helped me out, he made a par."

As talented as he was at golf, Tom also played football and basketball in high school, and stayed away from the course between the end of summer and the next spring. He was following the example of his father, who seldom played in the fall, preferring to spend his free time hunting in that time of year. (Winter golf was out of the question in Missouri, of course.)

When it came down to choosing a college, Watson followed in his father's footsteps and headed west to go to Stanford, as did Tom's two brothers, one older and one younger. The late 1960s was a tumultuous time on college campuses, and hailing from a country club background in America's heartland, Watson told *Sports Illustrated* he "was somewhat of a fish out of water" at Stanford.

He might have been conflicted at times about the clash of generations — he later admitted to voting for George McGovern for president in 1972, to which his father said, "You're an idiot" — but he ended up square on the side of his father's generation. During interviews he'll often comment on what's wrong with the way kids are raised and schooled today, and he gained a reputation as a voice of probity and old-time values in the 1990s when his letter to Augusta National helped get Gary McCord banned from the broadcast booth after he made a "bikini wax" reference.

One of the good things about going to Stanford was that the famed Pebble Beach Golf Links was about an hour-and-a-half drive to the south on the Monterey Peninsula. Watson made that trip about a dozen times during his college years after befriending starter Ray Parga, who allowed him to tee off before the first group in the morning. He doesn't remember breaking 75 in any of those rounds, but in 1982 he would go on to win the US Open on those links.

Just before entering Stanford, seventeen-year-old Tom had played a round at Pebble Beach with his father. He remembers his dad calling the eighth, ninth, and tenth holes "the best three par fours in a row in the world" and that they were randomly paired up with actors Imogene Coca and King Donovan.

While Watson was not a world-beater in college, he did earn an invitation to the Masters as an amateur in 1970. During that year's Christmas break when his friend David Wysong asked if he would follow his father into the insurance business, Tom answered, "I'm going to be the best player in the world."

Tom gave his father the news that he had decided to turn professional a few months later, while quail hunting in central Kansas. "Dad said just one thing," Tom recalls. "He said, 'Son, that's the right decision. Because if you didn't, you would always wonder if that's what you should have done.'"

Watson went on to win thirty-nine times on the PGA Tour, including eight majors. But he entered the eleventh season of his career without a victory in the US Open, a frustrating gap in his résumé, especially when you consider how much that championship meant to both Tom and Ray.

Ray could name every US Open winner going back to the championship's start in 1895, and instilled that sense of history to his son. "The Open became the pinnacle for me as well," Tom says, "very simply because it was the toughest tournament to win."

Watson finally scaled that mountain in 1982, when he chipped in for a birdie on the seventeenth hole of the final round then birdied the eighteenth for a two-stroke victory over Nicklaus at Pebble Beach. Watching at home, Ray later recalled, "That Sunday, all day long, my hands were so sweaty they were slimy. When Tommy made that pitch shot, I jumped four feet in the air."

For his part, Tom fondly remembers calling his dad after that victory, which came on Father's Day.

Proud as he was of his son and his accomplishments, the elder Watson never forgot how to apply the needle. When *Golf Digest* came to Kansas City for an interview in 1999, Ray was observed telling his son, who was struggling as his career on the regular PGA Tour wound down, "Tommy, you've got to make a cut."

Tom would win on the fifty-and-older Senior PGA Tour (now the Champions Tour) that fall, earning a spot in the MasterCard Championship in Hawaii in January 2000. Ray traveled there to watch Tom play, but died in Honolulu during the trip at the age of eighty.

Reflecting on the relationship, Tom says, "My dad was the foundation. He taught me to give nothing but my level best, and gave me a great example to follow. I've not only tried to pass that lesson down to my own son and daughter, but also to all kids that I come across."

Acknowledgments

This book could not have been completed without the generous interview time offered by players Brad Adamonis, Stewart Cink, Ray Floyd, Bill Haas, J.J. Henry, Peter Jacobsen, Christina Kim, Brittany Lincicome, Kristy McPherson, Kevin Streelman, and Tom Watson. I owe them my thanks, and also thanks to their fathers for inspiring their children.

Information from various magazine and newspaper articles was used to supplement the interviews. For the chapters on Phil Mickelson, Jack Nicklaus, and Arnold Palmer, in addition to articles, the following books were used as sources: *One Magical Sunday*, by Phil Mickelson with Donald T. Phillips; *Endurance: Winning Life's Majors the Phil Mickelson Way*, by David Magee; *The Greatest Game of All: My Life in Golf*, by Jack Nicklaus with Herbert Warren Wind; *Jack Nicklaus: My Story*, by Jack Nicklaus with Ken Bowden; *Jack Nicklaus: Memories and Mementos from Golf's Golden Bear*, by Jack Nicklaus; *Nicklaus*, by Mark Shaw; *Go For Broke*, by Arnold Palmer; *A Golfer's Life*, by Arnold Palmer with James Dodson; and *Arnie: The Evolution of a Legend*, by Mark H. McCormack.

At Skyhorse Publishing, thanks go to Mark Weinstein not only for his editing but also for supplying the idea for this book.

On the home front, thanks to my wife, Ludmila, for her support and my children Michael and Sophia for letting me get this done in my home office. And for bringing me up right and setting a good example, thanks to my mother, Virginia, and my late Dad, Dave Sr.

About the Author

Ron Ramsey

David Barrett has been a professional golf writer for three decades. For eighteen years, Barrett served as a features editor at *Golf* magazine, where he coordinated the magazine's major championship coverage. He presently has his own Web site, davidhbarrett.com, which is part of TheAPosition.com, and contributes to GolfObserver.com. The author of four previous books on golf, including *Miracle at Merion*, he lives in White Plains, New York.

Index